MW00615503

"This work is a ⸱
Biblical evaluation of Calvinism. Wilkin weighs
Calvinism in the balance of twelve key New Testament
verses and finds it to be wanting. In fairness, the book
includes an appendix listing responses by Calvinists to
these verses. Scholars and non-scholars alike will find
Wilkin's work helpful."

—*David L. Allen, PhD*
Dean, School of Preaching, SWBTS
Forth Worth, TX

"Bob Wilkin examines the Five Points of Calvinism, a
system developed over fifty years after Calvin's death. He
brings up many verses and arguments not usually found
in discussions on Reformed theology. Anyone interested
in Calvinism should have this book on his or her shelf."

—*David R. Anderson, PhD*
President, Grace School of Theology
The Woodlands, TX

"Concise, clear, and straight to the point! By using twelve
clear New Testament texts, Wilkin shows why each and
every point of the Calvinistic TULIP acrostic is Biblically
incorrect."

—*Anthony B. Badger, ThD*
Author of *Confronting Calvinism*
Lancaster, PA

"I applaud the tremendous effort by Dr. Wilkin to communicate in an irenic tone on a very polarizing subject. His great care in treating each verse with fairness and scholarship will benefit the reader's knowledge on this subject for years to come."

—Joseph M. Holden, PhD
President, Veritas Evangelical Seminary
Santa Ana, CA

"Let the Scriptures decide? Indeed they have! Wilkin has done it again. He has challenged the centuries old practice that assumes a theology and then looks for proof-texts to try to prove that theology."

—Stephen R. Lewis, PhD
President, Rocky Mountain Bible College & Seminary
Denver, CO

"Bob Wilkin shows that none of Calvinism's five (or six) points is Biblical. His contextual analysis of twelve key passages precludes Calvinism. These twelve are not the only ones barring Calvinism, but they make a good case for being a non-Calvinist."

—John H. Niemelä, PhD
President, Message of Life Ministries
Bennett, CO

Is Calvinism Biblical?

Let the Scriptures Decide

Is Calvinism Biblical?

Let the Scriptures Decide

Robert N. Wilkin

Grace Evangelical Society
Denton, Texas 76202

Is Calvinism Biblical? Let the Scriptures Decide

Copyright © 2017 by Grace Evangelical Society

Wilkin, Robert N., 1952—

ISBN 978-1-943399-22-2

All Scripture quotations, unless otherwise indicated,
are taken from The Holy Bible New King James
Version © 1982 by Thomas Nelson, Inc.

Requests for information should be
sent to our mailing address:

Grace Evangelical Society
P.O. Box 1308
Denton, TX 76202
www.faithalone.org
ges@faithalone.org

Design: Shawn C. Lazar

Printed in the United States of America.

*To the staff and supporters
of Grace Evangelical Society.*

Contents

Introduction

LET'S BEGIN BY SUMMARIZING what Calvinism is. In the rest of the book we will see whether Calvinism is consistent with the Word of God.

Calvinism, while named after John Calvin, is not a summary of what he taught. John Calvin died on May 27, 1564. Calvinism was essentially born in 1619 at the Synod of Dordt when Reformed theologians came up with five points which summarized their views on soteriology, the doctrine of salvation.

The synod was concerned about the teaching of a Reformed theologian named Jacobus Arminius. His followers have come to be called Arminians. Arminians believe that God gives people free will and that they are capable of both believing in Jesus and of falling away, thereby losing everlasting life.

There is no place in Scripture that mentions *the five points of Calvinism.* Each of the points can be evaluated in light of the meaning of many texts. That is what this book will do.

The five points are logically connected. They truly rise or fall together. The idea that someone could be a two-, three-, or four-point Calvinist is contrary to the system itself, though some four-point Calvinists today argue strongly that they are true Calvinists. Calvinism is an all-or-nothing system according to most of its adherents.

The five points are easily remembered by the acronym TULIP—especially since Calvinism has been strong in the Netherlands, famous for its tulips. Each of the letters of TULIP stands for the first word of one of the five points.

Since the subtitle of this book is *Let the Scriptures Decide*, you might think we will consider scores of passages. While that would be helpful, it would also be enormous. In order to keep this book at a reasonable size, I've selected two passages to discuss for each of Calvinism's points. A dozen passages serve as jurors to decide whether Calvinism is Biblical.

The T in TULIP stands for *total depravity*. That does not mean that men are sinful and unable to gain everlasting life by their own works. Instead, it means much more, i.e., that the unregenerate are like rocks or cadavers. The unregenerate have no ability to respond to God at all. None.

A famous Calvinist illustration concerns a corpse at the bottom of a well. Would-be rescuers, not knowing the man is dead, throw a rope down and shout for the man to tie it around his waist so that they can pull him up and save him. However, since the man is a cadaver, he is unable to do anything. He cannot hear what they are saying, move his arms, or tie the rope around his waist.

Likewise, it is claimed, the unregenerate are hopeless and helpless. You can share God's Word with them 24/7 and it will have no impact because they are spiritual cadavers, incapable of understanding or believing what you say.

How then can anyone possibly be born again if this is true? The logical solution in Calvinism is that regeneration precedes faith. In order for a person to be able to believe, he must first be born again. While most Calvinists say the new birth occurs just a fraction of a second before faith occurs, some Calvinists say that regeneration can occur months, years, or even decades before faith occurs. In this view, God guarantees that those whom He has regenerated will not die before they come to faith.

Two passages which we will consider which evaluate the Calvinist understanding of total depravity are John 6:35 and Acts 10:4.

The U in TULIP stands for *unconditional election*. This means that God had no reason to choose certain people over others. He simply elected some and did not elect others. Calvinism says that unconditional election is a loving choice since there is nothing whatsoever in the ones elected that led God to choose them.

We will look at Acts 13:46 and John 5:39-40 in order to see if the Calvinist view of unconditional election is consistent with Scripture.

The L in TULIP stands for *limited atonement*. In this view, Christ died for only the elect. Thus the rest of humanity is doomed not only because they are not elect, but also because the blood of Christ does not take away their sins.

A Calvinist could not in good conscience say to a person, "God loves you and has a wonderful plan for your life." Why not? Because the Calvinist knows that Christ did not die for a huge percentage of people.

We will evaluate limited atonement in light of John 1:29 and 2 Pet 2:1.

The I in TULIP refers to *irresistible grace.* This does not mean that God's grace is wonderfully appealing to those who are open to it. Remember that in Calvinism until a person is regenerated, he is a cadaver and has no ability to respond. And only the elect are regenerated.

So irresistible grace means that anyone God is drawing to Himself will not be able to resist. God's grace is effective in bringing all for whom Christ died, the elect, to faith in Christ before they die. This is not because the person was responsive to God's drawing. (Remember, people are cadavers.) This is because regeneration precedes faith and God's drawing of those whom He has regenerated inevitably leads them to faith in Christ.

Passages which we will consider related to Calvinism's doctrine of irresistible grace are John 12:32 and Matt 23:37-39.

The P in Calvinism is a bit misleading. Typically it is understood to refer to the *perseverance of the saints.* However, it is also said to refer to the *preservation of the saints.*

Probably we should understand there to be *six points of Calvinism*, points that spell TULIPP.

In 1963, Steele and Thomas wrote a book called *The Five Points of Calvinism.* Then in 2004, twenty-three years after Steele died, Thomas joined with Quinn and they released a revised version of the book. In the preface they say this about the fifth point of Calvinism:

In the first edition of the book, in the section dealing with "The Perseverance of the Saints or the Security of Believers," our primary emphasis was on God's *preservation*, and hence our security as believers, rather than on the believer's *perseverance*. This distinction is now highlighted because there are many who profess to be Christians, but give little or no evidence of a changed life…We are not only *preserved* by God for salvation, but required by Him to *persevere* in the faith, striving continually toward a holy life. Without our *perseverance*, we can have no assurance of His *preservation*.[1]

In the appendix of the second edition they have this to add about the fifth point of Calvinism, "One could almost speak of the six points of Calvinism, the *fifth* point being the *preservation* of the saints and the *sixth* point being the *perseverance* of the saints."[2] They quote A. N. Martin: "'The only proof I have [that] he preserves me is that by his grace, I am enabled to persevere.'"[3]

The perseverance of the saints is the teaching that all who have been regenerated and then given the gift of faith in Christ will persevere in faith and good works until death, though there might be short times of rebellion against the Lord. Thus no one who died as an alcoholic, drug addict, adulterer, or liar is truly born again.

---

[1] David N. Steele, Curtis C. Thomas, and S. Lance Quinn, *The Five Points of Calvinism: Defined, Defended, and Documented*, Second Edition (Phillipsburg, NJ: P & R Publishing, 1963, 2004), xviii, italics theirs.
[2] Ibid., 148-49, emphasis theirs.
[3] Ibid., 149.

Of course, since no one is perfect, and since according to Calvinism only perfect people could be sure they would persevere, Calvinists believe and teach that no one can be sure of his eternal destiny until he dies. As one leading Calvinist pastor and seminary professor told me, "I cannot be sure that I will persevere. If I do not, then I will prove that what I thought were the works of the Spirit through me were not, and I will prove that I was never born again in the first place. I would thus end up in the lake of fire."

The perseverance of the saints will be weighed in light of Luke 8:11-13 and John 4:13-15, the subjects of Chapters 9 and 10.

The preservation of the saints is sometimes called *eternal security,* or *once saved, always saved.* In Calvinism, this does not simply mean that all who are born again are eternally secure, as is commonly thought. Rather, this means that *all who persevere* are eternally secure. We know that we are saved by persevering until death in faith and good works.

With the exception of some maverick Calvinists—like David Engelsma or Randall Zachman, no one in a Calvinist church, not even the pastor, is sure he himself is eternally secure. The pastor cannot be sure that he is secure. Nor can he be sure that his wife, or his children, or his elders are secure in Christ. That is because security is not linked to those who believe in Christ, but to those who persevere in both faith and good works. (By contrast, Calvinists like Engelsma and Zachman link assurance to faith in Christ, apart from works.)

In discussing the Calvinist understanding of perseverance, George Bryson says,

> The Calvinist doctrine of perseverance of the
> saints allows for a formal recognition of a true
> believer's security of salvation. And yet accord-
> ing to Calvinism, no true believer can have
> assurance of salvation because full assurance
> cannot come until you arrive at the end of your
> earthly sojourn.[4]

Calvinism has something called *temporary faith*
and even *temporary works*. Thus people can believe in
Christ *for a time*, and yet be unregenerate. That is puz-
zling since Calvinism teaches that unregenerate are like
cadavers, and they can't believe. But they make an exception when discussing certain passages which speak of
people who believe for a time and then during a season
of temptation fall away (e.g., Luke 8:13). Contrary to the
Calvinist understanding of total depravity, most Calvinists teach that unregenerate people can do the types of
works that the regenerate do *for a time*. That is another
reason why assurance is impossible for the Calvinist.

What this means practically is that Calvinism is
a lifetime of *personal evangelism*. By that I mean that
Calvinists are *evangelizing themselves* their entire lives.
Calvinists remind themselves daily that only by persevering in faith and good works will they make it into the
kingdom. They constantly warn themselves about the
possibility of temporary faith and temporary works.

It is true that God preserves believers. But is it true
that He preserves them in the way Calvinists suggest?
Revelation 20:11-15 and John 11:25-27 (Chapters 11

---

[4] George Bryson, *The Dark Side of Calvinism* (Santa Ana, CA: Calvary
Chapel Publishing, 2004), 268.

and 12) will be considered as we evaluate the Calvinist understanding of the preservation of the saints.

If you are reading this and you are a Calvinist, my hope is that you will search the Scriptures to see if these things are so (Acts 17:11). After all, it is Scripture, not the writings of men, upon which our faith must be built.

George Bryson summarizes Calvinism's five points in this short statement: "You will be saved or damned for all eternity because you were saved or damned from all eternity."[5] While Calvinists might quibble with that summary, they would acknowledge that Bryson correctly captures Calvinism's conviction that one's eternal destiny was determined by God before He created the heavens and the earth and Adam and Eve. Nothing anyone can do can change that, though Calvinists live as though their eternal destiny depended on them, not on God. Practically speaking, Calvinists are trying hard to make it into God's kingdom.

If you are not a Calvinist, I hope you are persuaded that if you believe in Christ today, then you are secure forever. Even temporary faith results in eternal salvation. Of course, believing in Christ is more than believing He exists. I will lay out in this book what it means to believe in Christ. But the good news is that you can know if you believe in Him, and if you do, you can know you are secure forever.

Some believe that the five points of Calvinism unintentionally present a very unflattering view of God. Roger Olson wrote a book against Calvinism in part

---

[5] George L. Bryson, *The Five Points of Calvinism: Weighed and Found Wanting* (Costa Mesa, CA: The Word for Today, 1996), 121.

because "I want people to think better about God than Calvinism allows."[6]

Calvinism is well intentioned. But is it consistent with Scripture? Let the Scriptures decide!

---

[6] Roger E. Olson, *Against Calvinism* (Grand Rapids, MI: Zondervan, 2011), 179.

SECTION 1

Total Depravity

CHAPTER 1

Faith Precedes Regeneration (John 6:35)

ONE OF THE MAIN ASPECTS of the Calvinist understanding of total depravity—the T in TULIP—is that regeneration precedes faith. Unfortunately, most Evangelicals do not know what that means and so they are likely to accept the first point of Calvinism, thinking that total depravity means that we are all sinners and that we are not able to save ourselves (Rom 3:23). But total depravity means much more than that.

While most Evangelicals say that one must believe in Jesus in order to be born again (i.e., regenerate), by contrast, Calvinists say that one must be born again (i.e., regenerate) in order to believe.

While most Calvinists say that regeneration and faith occur almost simultaneously, they all say that regeneration must precede faith since they do not believe that spiritually dead people can believe.

It should be noted that there are some Calvinists who freely say that regeneration might precede faith by quite a long period of time. One Calvinist writer tells of a man who he believes came to faith 65 years after he was born again![1] The man supposedly was a born-again *unbeliever* for over six decades.

The Bread of Life Illustration

John 6:35 is a show stopper for the first point of Calvinism.

After Jesus fed over 5,000 men (plus many women and children), many came to Him and asked Him to give them an ongoing supply of bread: "Lord, give us this bread always" (John 6:34). Sadly, they were thinking in purely physical terms.[2] The feeding of the 5,000 was not a lesson about social security, but eternal security.

They had previously referred to the fact that "our fathers ate the manna in the desert; as it is written, '*He gave them bread from heaven to eat*'" (John 6:31). They wanted that miracle repeated daily.

Jesus' first words after their request were, "I am the bread of life." Clearly the Lord was continuing the illustration of bread, and even bread that comes from heaven, since He Himself had come down from heaven.

But when Jesus referred to *life* in the expression "I am the bread of life," He was not referring to *physical* life.

[1] Stephen E. Smallman, *Spiritual Birthline: Understanding How We Experience the New Birth* (Wheaton, IL: Crossway Books, 2006), 22-23. Smallman likens the new birth to physical birth. He says conception occurs long before birth physically and typically spiritually as well.
[2] The response of the woman at the well regarding the living water was nearly identical. Compare John 4:15. She too was thinking in purely physical terms (as was Nicodemus in John 3:4).

Instead, He was referring to *spiritual* life, to *everlasting* life. This is clear by what He said next.

The One Who Comes to Jesus Will Never Hunger

He then said, "He who comes to Me shall never hunger." Remember, they were asking about a continuous supply of bread from heaven. The Lord promised something better. He had promised the woman at the well that one drink would forever quench her thirst (John 4:14). Now He said that one act of partaking of the bread of life, that is, coming to Him, means that a person would never hunger again. As with the living water, the bread of life once received results in everlasting life that can never be lost. The words *shall never hunger* are figurative. They mean that the one who believes in Jesus is secure forever. The life that *the Bread of Life* gives is that kind of life, everlasting life.

Calvinists agree that coming to Jesus in John 6:35 refers to believing in Him,[3] and that *shall never hunger* refers to eternal security.[4]

Coming to Jesus, that is, believing in Him, *precedes*

---

[3] See John F. MacArthur, Jr., *The Gospel According to Jesus*, Revised and Expanded Anniversary Edition (Grand Rapids, MI: Zondervan, 1988, 1994, 2008), 121. "In John 6:35…to come to Jesus is to believe in Him." See also John Piper, "Letter to a Friend Concerning the So-Called Lordship Salvation," DesiringGod.org, Feb 1, 1990, s.v., "The Nature of Faith in the Gospel of John." Last accessed August 18, 2017.

[4] See D. A. Carson, *The Gospel According to John* (Grand Rapids, MI: Eerdmans, 1991), 288. See also Pastor Steve Swets at Reformedfellowship. net, June 1, 2016, "'I am the Bread of Life': A Devotional on John 6:35." Swets says, "What this means is that those who eat of the Bread of Life will live because He lives. Two senses are given: in verse 56 is a picture of remaining united, and then in verse 57 is a picture of Jesus being the source of life. Similar to a root and branches, so is the bread of life and

never hungering. One must partake of the bread of life before he gets the life. The Calvinist idea that one gets the life and then eats of the bread of life is contradicted by this text.

The One Who Believes in Him Will Never Thirst

The Lord next picked up a metaphor He used earlier with the woman at the well (John 4:10-14), except this time He stripped away the first part of the metaphor.

Instead of saying, "He who drinks the living water will never thirst," the Lord said, "He who believes in Me shall never thirst." He interpreted for us what it means to drink the living water. It is believing in Him. And we know from John 4:14-15 that the Lord was not speaking of continuous lifelong drinking. The moment a person drinks the living water—that is, the moment he believes in Jesus—he will never thirst again. The words *shall never thirst* clearly mean *shall never die spiritually, shall never perish.* The one who believes in Jesus *has everlasting life that can never be lost.*

Once again, regeneration does not precede faith. The very moment one believes in Jesus, he is given everlasting life. Not before.

Eternal Security Is for All Who Believe

People like to go to the Apostle Paul to prove eternal security. Although Paul certainly does teach that doctrine (e.g., Rom 4:4-5; 8:31-39; Eph 2:8-9), the Lord

---

those who partake of the bread of life. What happens is that they are filled; they live life forevermore. Though they may die, yet they will live."

taught it first. John 6:35 is arguably the simplest and most powerful eternal security verse in the Bible. It is elegant in its simplicity and power. The one who believes in Him shall never hunger and shall never thirst. Never. Once we partake of the bread of life, we will never need to partake again to be eternally secure. Once we drink of the living water, we will never need to drink again in order to have a secure eternal destiny.

Of course, this too is a contradiction of Calvinism. According to Calvinism, God only preserves (guarantees the eternal destiny of) those who persevere in faith and good works. That is the fifth point of Calvinism, preservation for the saints who persevere. But the Lord of glory promises something much different—to preserve all who simply believe in Him—with no perseverance required.

Faith Precedes Regeneration

I don't know who came up with the idea that regeneration precedes faith, but I know that Calvinists embrace that idea and proclaim it boldly.

Why Calvinism hasn't fixed this obvious error I don't know. I suppose it is because Calvinism is a construct of ideas that rise or fall together. If Calvinists were to give in on this point, I suppose the whole system would collapse. So they hang on to a position that stands in direct opposition to the clear teaching of Scripture.

Don't get me wrong. Their view that regeneration precedes faith is possible. God *could* have set it up that way (if faith were not a condition of regeneration). But that is not what the Bible teaches. If what the Bible teaches contradicts my position, however logical the system may seem, then I should submit to the Scriptures.

After all, it is also possible that faith precedes regeneration. The only way that it would be illogical is if the Calvinist understanding of spiritual deadness (i.e., total depravity) were correct. But it is not.

After I graduated from seminary I called myself a Calvinist for nearly two decades. For me the key point of Calvinism was the preservation of the saints. I thought my belief in eternal security made me a Calvinist. But I came to see that I do not believe in any of the five points as taught by Calvinism. Sure, I could manipulate the meaning of all five points and say I believed them, but that would not really make me a Calvinist.

For the last fifteen years or so I simply say I am a Biblicist. I believe the Bible. I am not a Calvinist or an Arminian. The Bible is enough for me.

Faith in Christ is the condition of everlasting life. One must believe in Jesus in order to be born again. Therefore, faith precedes regeneration. And that means the T in TULIP is false, at least, as it is explained by Calvinism.

So when you evangelize, call people to believe in Jesus for everlasting life. Tell them that whoever comes to Jesus will never hunger and whoever believes in Him will never thirst. The Lord Jesus guarantees the eternal destiny of all who believe in Him. Because of the cross of Christ, our sins and our works are not the issue. The only issue is whether or not we believe in Him for what He promises. If we do, then we have everlasting life that can never be lost.

John 6:35 shows that Calvinism is inconsistent with the Bible.

CHAPTER 2

The Unregenerate Can Respond to God (Acts 10:4)

CALVINISTS THINK OF UNREGENERATE people as cadavers. That is, they see them as totally unable to respond to God in a saving way—or in any way.

They often cite Rom 3:11 which says, "There is none who seeks after God." Yet we know from many texts that what Paul means is that no one seeks after God *of his own initiative*. But God does take the initiative (John 12:32; 16:7-11; Acts 17:27), gives natural revelation to all (Rom 1:19-20), and convicts all of sin, righteousness, and judgment (John 16:7-11).

Cornelius is exhibit A (though there are many examples like him in Scripture). He sought God *before* he was born again because God was first seeking him. If our theology does not allow for the unregenerate to respond to God, then we ought to change our theology.

Cornelius Was Not Yet Born Again
(Acts 10:44; 11:14)

I suppose some might object that Cornelius must already have been born again. I remember the president of a seminary suggesting that to me. He reasoned this way:

Major Premise:	Only born-again people can seek God.
Minor Premise:	Cornelius sought God.
Conclusion:	Cornelius was born again when he sought God.

However, after I showed him what I'm about to show you, he changed his mind. He decided that Cornelius was unregenerate before Peter preached to him. I don't know how he resolved that with his Calvinism, but he saw the point.

In Acts 11:13-14 Peter related something that Cornelius told him. This statement was not given by Luke in Chapter 10. Peter reported that Cornelius "told us how he had seen an angel standing in his house, who said to him, 'Send men to Joppa, and call for Simon whose surname is Peter, who will tell you words by which you and your household will be saved.'" While the word *saved* refers to regeneration only about 30% of the time in the New Testament, this is one of those times. One way we know that is by what we learn in Acts 10:44.

Peter preached Christ to Cornelius and his household. In Acts 10:43, Luke tells us what Peter said: "To Him all the prophets witness that, through His name, whoever believes in Him will receive remission of sins." It is unlikely that this was the intended ending of his sermon. Peter may have planned to add more information, including mention that along with forgiveness comes regeneration/salvation.

However, verse 44 says, "While Peter was still speaking these words, the Holy Spirit fell upon all those who heard the word." The words *while Peter was still speaking these words* imply that Peter had not finished.

But Cornelius and his household had been told in advance that Peter would give him words by which he and his household *would be saved* (Acts 11:14). Thus when they heard that all who believe in Jesus receive the remission of sins, they knew that Peter was speaking of something which accompanies salvation. At that moment they were convinced that all who believe in Jesus are saved forever. When they believed, they received the Holy Spirit. The reception of the Spirit occurred when they were born again.

Cornelius was unregenerate when he sought the Lord with alms and prayers. And, as we shall now see, the Lord actually took note of his prayers and his giving. His example shows that the unregenerate can respond to God. Thus the T in TULIP is contradicted by the Biblical account concerning Cornelius.

Cornelius's Prayers and Alms Pleased God (Acts 10:4)

Pastor Bailey Smith once famously said that God does not hear the prayers of Jews. He meant that God does not hear the prayers of unbelievers and that unless a Jewish person believed in Jesus, God did not hear his prayers either.

But God does hear the prayers of unbelievers. Cornelius, a Gentile who worshipped in a Jewish synagogue, got prayers through to God: "So he [an angel] said to him [Cornelius], 'Your prayers and your alms have come up for a memorial before God'" (Acts 10:4).

The word translated *memorial* (*mnēmosunon*, used only here and Matt 26:13 and Mark 14:9) refers to something remembered, especially "an offering that presents a worshipper to God" (BDAG, p. 655).[1] In other words, his prayers and alms pleased God. They got His attention in a good way.

Acts 10:35 bears out this understanding: "But in every nation whoever fears Him and works righteousness is accepted by Him." Cornelius feared God. Luke had already told us in Acts 10:2 that he was "…a devout man and one who feared God with all his household." But now Peter added that Cornelius worked righteousness.

That saying has confused many. How can the unregenerate *work righteousness*? The confusion derives from Calvinism's understanding of total depravity.

We know from Isa 64:6 that unbelievers produce righteous deeds: "All our righteousnesses are like filthy rags…" That means the Jewish people to whom Isaiah was writing, many of whom were unbelievers, did righteous deeds, but they had no merit with God. Their deeds were like filthy rags before Him.

Unbelievers still have the image of God. Thus some of His attributes (called His *communicable* attributes) are evident in all humans, believers and unbelievers alike. These attributes include love, justice, kindness, and

---

[1] Arndt, William F., and Gingrich, F. Wilbur, *A Greek English Lexicon of the New Testament and Other Early Christian Literature* (Chicago, IL: The University of Chicago Press, 2000). Hereafter, BDAG.

mercy. Even though we all fall short of God's glory (Rom 3:23), we are nonetheless still in His image (cf. Gen 1:26-27; 1 Cor 11:7; Jas 3:9). The Spirit of God can work in the lives of the unregenerate. Thus they can "work righteousness," though those righteous deeds, like alms and prayers, have no merit with God. God is not obligated to give everlasting life to those who work righteousness, since all fall short of God's glory (Rom 3:23). But He is obligated to "accept" them. What Peter meant is that the person who works righteousness will receive more light, more revelation, from God. Peter was the messenger of that revelation in this case.

Cornelius Understood and Obeyed God's Communication to Him from an Angel (Acts 10:1-8)

According to Calvinism's understanding of total depravity, Cornelius was like a cadaver or a stone, incapable of understanding or responding to anything God said. And yet, according to the Bible, Cornelius did understand and respond to what God said.

God told him to send to Joppa for Simon Peter. Cornelius immediately understood and obeyed.

Have you had an unbeliever attend your Bible study or church? What you find is that unbelievers can indeed understand and learn. If the lesson is on the Rapture, they can understand it and even come to believe it. If it is about God's eternality, they can understand and believe. If it is about the promise of everlasting life to the believer, they can grasp that, too, and believe. And if they do, then we say that the person in question was born again that day.

The reason it is not futile to allow unbelievers to attend your Bible study or church is because unbelievers can understand and respond to God's Word. Cornelius certainly did.

The Actions of Cornelius Resulted in His Hearing the Message of Life (Acts 10:30-43)

Did God sovereignly and miraculously send Peter to Cornelius? Absolutely. He first sent an angel to Cornelius himself, then gave Peter three visions to convince him to go to Cornelius. God did exactly what was necessary to bring the promise of everlasting life to Cornelius and his household.

God's sovereignty does not mean that the unregenerate cannot respond to God. Cornelius responded to the light God gave him, and as a result, God sent him Peter and the message of everlasting life.

Steve Douglass, President of Campus Crusade for Christ, wrote concerning Cornelius:

> Even before coming to understand about Jesus, he was a devout person who feared God, gave generously to those in need, and prayed regularly...The huge impact of what happened through Cornelius didn't unfold until the Council of Jerusalem in Acts 15...Peter stood up and validated spreading the gospel to the Gentiles...God could have used other people and methods to open that door. But He chose to use Cornelius. Why? At least in part, because

his life was a light for God, shining brightly to all around.[2]

Cornelius Believed and Then Was Born Again (Acts 10:43-44)

The order we find here is faith first, then regeneration. That is the same order found in the rest of the Bible. Of course, this too violates one aspect of the T in TULIP, the idea that regeneration precedes faith.

Cornelius believed (see Peter's summary in Acts 15:7-9), and then the Holy Spirit fell upon him. If the Calvinist position were true, Luke would have to say the opposite.

Of course, Acts 11:14 confirms this understanding: "Peter…will tell you words by which you and your household will be saved." Notice the words that Peter spoke led to their salvation. They were only saved once they believed those words.

The Unregenerate Can Respond to God

In Acts, Cornelius is not the only example of someone seeking God. Lydia in Acts 16 was also a God-fearer and she, too, sought God. She was at the place of prayer by the riverside when Paul came and spoke.

Likewise, the more noble-minded Jews of Berea (Acts 17:11) "searched the Scriptures daily to see if these things [the things spoken by Paul about Jesus] were true."

---

[2] Steve Douglass, "Where My Heart Is..." *Connection* (October 2017): 1-2.

Lastly, Paul told the Athenian philosophers, "And He has made from one blood every nation of men...so that they should seek the Lord, in the hope that they might grope for Him and find Him, though He is not far from each one of us" (Acts 17:26-27).

Calvinism says that the unregenerate cannot respond to God. That is incorrect. The unregenerate can respond to God.

Acts 10:4 contradicts Calvinism and the Calvinist position on total depravity.

SECTION 2

Unconditional Election

CHAPTER 3

People Judge Themselves Worthy or Unworthy of Everlasting Life (Acts 13:46)

> Then Paul and Barnabas grew bold and said, "It was necessary that the word of God should be spoken to you first; but since you reject it, and judge yourselves unworthy of everlasting life, behold, we turn to the Gentiles."

GOD IS SOVEREIGN. That is, He rules the world and the universe. Everything is under His control.

Calvinism exalts God's sovereignty, which is a good thing. But Calvinism's view of unconditional election attributes to God something which is not true. Calvinism says that God arbitrarily selected a small percentage of people to spend eternity in His kingdom and passed over the rest, dooming them to eternal condemnation. The reprobate have been doomed from before the creation, before they sinned, or even existed. There is

39

nothing they can do about their fate. They are going to be tormented in the lake of fire forever. They cannot seek God. They cannot come to faith in Christ. They cannot be born again.

Unconditional Election Says God Sovereignly Determines Who Will Have Everlasting Life

According to Calvinism, God chose who would have everlasting life before creation. I was taught in seminary the illustration of a large ball of clay. Imagine a ball of clay the size of a beach ball. Now imagine pinching off a small piece the size of a golf ball.

The golf ball size piece of clay represents the elect, those who will have everlasting life. The beach ball size of clay represents those not chosen, those who will spend eternity in the lake of fire.

Calvinism teaches that the non-elect have no opportunity to have everlasting life. They are doomed even before they are conceived or before they draw their first breath. In addition, Calvinism teaches that God made this decision unconditionally. That is, He did not look in advance and see which ones would be more responsive, or which ones would freely come to faith in Christ, or anything of the kind. God simply chose.

That sounds arbitrary.

Calvinists reject that charge because it sounds uncaring. It sounds like God just arbitrarily pulled out, say, 1% of humanity, and the rest He passed over.

Yet while Calvinists reject the charge that election is arbitrary, the term *unconditional* conveys that idea. If God indeed chose some and not others to be born again, and if His choice had nothing to do with the people chosen or not chosen, then God's election was arbitrary and unfair.

Roger Olson makes this insightful comment about unconditional election:

> A conundrum…is the Calvinist belief that God selects some people to save and others to "pass over" and that this selection has absolutely nothing to do with anything he sees in them or about them. Yet his selection is not arbitrary…There is no middle ground between arbitrary and there being something about people that causes God to select them (such as a free response to God's invitation to be saved). An appeal to mystery is incorrect; this is not a mystery but a conundrum.[1]

This point of Calvinism may seem logical, but it is contradicted by Acts 13:46.

Paul Says People Determine Whether They Will Have Everlasting Life (Acts 13:46)

On his first missionary journey Paul went to southern Galatia. There he and Barnabas led many to faith in Christ and planted churches in a number of cities including Lystra, Iconium, Derbe, and Pisidian Antioch.

Acts 13:46 is part of Luke's first report of an evangelistic message that Paul gave. That message occurred in the synagogue in Pisidian Antioch.

---

[1] Roger E. Olson, *Against Calvinism* (Grand Rapids, MI: Zondervan, 2011), 178.

A huge crowd had turned out to hear Paul and Barnabas. They had persuaded "many of the Jews and devout proselytes" the previous Sabbath (Acts 13:43). However, this time "when the Jews saw the multitudes, they were filled with envy; and contradicting and blaspheming, they opposed the things spoken by Paul" (v 45).

These unbelievers were not merely rejecting the message of life. They were trying to keep others from believing it as well.

Paul and Barnabas rebuked them, saying that they had chosen not to be open to the words of everlasting life. Thus God was sending Paul and Barnabas to speak to the Gentiles (v 46). Verse 48 shows that those Gentiles were open to the message of life.

If the Calvinist position on election were true, then Paul would not have said, "You judge yourselves unworthy of everlasting life," but something like, "God did not choose you to have everlasting life," or "God determined before time began that you would spend eternity in the lake of fire," or "It is impossible for people like you to have everlasting life because you were not chosen by God."

Of course, the people to whom Paul was speaking were, for the most part, God's chosen people, i.e., Jews. (There were some Gentile God-fearers present, but they would have been a decided minority in a synagogue.) Jews are God's chosen people, so the Calvinist interpretation of verse 46 would not have made sense to them.

But Paul didn't say they were doomed because God did not choose them for everlasting life. In fact, he said the opposite. Paul said that *they themselves*, not God, judged themselves unworthy of everlasting life.

The Apostle Paul was not a Calvinist. His theology places responsibility on the listeners. Whether they believe or not depends on their openness, not on some determination made by God.

Luke Says the Unregenerate Are Able to Respond to the Message of Life

There were many Jewish and Gentile believers at the time Paul spoke at the synagogue in Pisidian Antioch. Paul himself was a prime example of a Jew who came to faith in Christ for everlasting life (cf. 1 Tim 1:16), as was Barnabas.

Likewise, many unregenerate Gentiles came to faith in Christ and gained everlasting life at that time (Acts 13:48). They heard the same message, but unlike those who rejected the message without prayer or seeking the Scriptures (cf. Acts 17:11), they *inclined themselves toward* the message (that is what the words *hosoi ēsan tetagmenoi*, typically translated *as many as had been appointed*, means in Acts 13:48)[2] and as a result believed it.

Terry Carter, who is neither a Free Grace advocate nor a Calvinist, lays out the differences between the Jews who rejected everlasting life in verse 46 and the Gentiles who accepted everlasting life in verse 48:[3]

---

[2] See, Bob Wilkin, "A New View on Acts 13:48: 'As Many as Were Prepared for Eternal Life Believed," *Grace in Focus*, Jan-Feb 2007. It can be found at https://faithalone.org/magazine/y2007/2jan07.html.

[3] "Does Acts 13:48 Teach Calvinism?" *The Gospel Unashamed*, April 2015, p. 2. It can be found at the summit.org website under Current and Past Articles.

Jews (Acts 13:45-46)	Gentiles (Acts 13:48)
• Filled with envy, contradicted.	• Were glad.
• Blasphemed and opposed Paul; rejected the Word of God.	• Glorified the Word of the Lord.
• Judged themselves unworthy of everlasting life.	• Determined themselves for everlasting life.
• Refused to believe.	• Believed.

The unregenerate certainly are capable of judging themselves unworthy of everlasting life. But the unregenerate are also capable of being inclined to everlasting life.[4] All who are so inclined will hear the message of life and believe it.

Dave Hunt cites various translations, grammarians, and commentators who variously translate *tetagmenoi* in Acts 13:48 as follows: as many as *wanted, had become disposed, were disposed,* and *were determined.*[5] The ones who believed were Gentiles who wanted or were disposed to receive everlasting life.

Anthony Badger contrasts the response of the Gentiles who believed in Acts 13:48 and the Jews who rejected Christ in Acts 13:46:

---

[4] Carter suggests that the readers were determined to have everlasting life. That is, unlike the Jews of Acts 13:46 who were closed to the message, these Gentiles were open to the message of everlasting life. They were attracted, rather than repulsed, by the message of everlasting life for those who believe in Jesus.

[5] Dave Hunt, *What Love Is This? Calvinism's Misrepresentation of God,* Second Edition (Bend, OR: The Berean Call, 2004), 263-65.

> The Jews, *having judged themselves* (middle voice) *unworthy* of eternal life in 13:46, did not believe and receive it. Their internal disposition was against the message that promised eternal life...In 13:47-48 the *Gentiles*, having heard of the availability of eternal life, rejoiced, received the Lord's message, and believed for salvation.[6]

He went on to suggest that *tetagmenoi* in Acts 13:48 refers to people who "had given themselves to eternal life,"[7] and "who desire[d] to live forever."[8] He sees the issue as one's "internal disposition" toward the message and toward everlasting life.

Acts 13:46 Contradicts Unconditional Election

I find it odd that many Calvinists will point to Acts 13:48 as a proof text for unconditional election. Even if Acts 13:48 taught unconditional election (which it does not), Acts 13:46 directly contradicts it.

Paul rebuked many of his listeners, people who were fellow Jews: "You reject it," he said. That is, *you reject the message of everlasting life.* "You judge yourselves unworthy of everlasting life," Paul charged. What a tragedy. The Messiah had come and His own people—for the most part—rejected Him and the life which He freely gives (cf. John 1:11-13).

George Bryson points out, "Even the Calvinist must concede that unbelievers are addressed in Scripture

---

[6] Anthony B. Badger, *Confronting Calvinism* (Columbia, SC: NP, 2013), 202, emphases his.
[7] Ibid., 201.
[8] Ibid., 202.

in a way that makes unbelief seem avoidable and self-imposed."[9] Acts 13:46 is one such passage.

No Calvinist would say today what Paul said in Acts 13:46 because it contradicts Calvinism.

Acts 13:46 is reminiscent of the Lord's rebuke of His self-righteous Jewish listeners in John 5:39-40, a passage we will consider in the next chapter.

---

[9] George L. Bryson, *The Five Points of Calvinism: Weighed and Found Wanting* (Costa Mesa, CA: The Word for Today, 1996), 92.

CHAPTER 4

People Not Willing to Come to Jesus for Everlasting Life (John 5:39-40)

"You search the Scriptures, for in them you think you have eternal life, and these are they which testify of Me. But you are not willing to come to Me that you may have life."

MANY IF NOT MOST Old Testament scholars today say that there was no concept of everlasting life by those who read and believed the Old Testament. The same view is held by most New Testament scholars as well.

John 5:39-40 shows that claim to be false. The Lord Jesus was speaking with very religious, yet unbelieving, Jews. The Church Age obviously had not yet begun when Jesus was conducting His ministry. The Lord was speaking to Jews living under the Law of Moses. While John 5:39-40 is found in the New Testament and is written to people during the Church Age, it reports on a time before Pentecost and the birth of the church. The people to whom Jesus spoke were Old Testament people.

The Lord said that they searched the Old Testament in order to find evidence that they have eternal life. They did not contradict Him. They did not say, "eternal life, what is that?"

What He said also contradicts the Calvinist view of unconditional election.

Jesus' Audience Thought That by Keeping the Commands They'd Have Everlasting Life (John 5:39)

When Jesus said "in them [the Old Testament] you think you have eternal life," He meant that the Pharisees and most Jews in His audience believed that by keeping the Law of Moses they would obtain entrance into the Messiah's kingdom. Zane Hodges comments on John 5:39 in his commentary on John 1-6:

> What is probably implied here is that the Jews are searching the Old Testament so as not to overlook any commandment that it contains (note the words "in them"). Their idea would be that by minutely keeping God's law they could obtain eternal life (note the lawyer's question in Luke 10:25).[1]

Now if they were stuck in that belief and unable to believe in Jesus, then the Calvinist view of election might

---

[1] Zane C. Hodges, *Faith in His Name: Listening to the Gospel of John* (Corinth, TX: Grace Evangelical Society, 2015), 116.

still be intact. (Of course, why are unregenerate people able to search the Scriptures? Can cadavers do that?) But what the Lord said next showed that they are able to understand and apply what He was saying.

The Old Testament Scriptures Testify That Jesus Is the Messiah And the Source of Life

Why bring up the Scriptures if an unregenerate person cannot understand or apply them? Why practice apologetics (the Scriptures testify that Jesus is the Savior and Messiah) on unregenerate people if they can't understand or be influenced?

True, there are some Calvinists who are evangelistic and who practice apologetics, but they are being inconsistent. But even among Calvinists who practice apologetics and evangelism, none would say that a non-elect person is capable of responding to the testimony of Scripture. Yet that is what the Lord showed in His words thus far. And what He went on to say is even more of a show stopper for Calvinism.

But Jesus' Listeners Were Unwilling to Come To Him (John 5:40)

Calvinists do not speak of willingness or unwillingness to believe in Christ[2] for everlasting life since, in their view, the unregenerate cannot be willing or unwilling to believe. The unregenerate are like rocks, with no spiritual sensitivity at all.

---

[2] In John's Gospel, *coming to Jesus* refers to believing in Him. In His Bread of Life discourse the Lord said, "He who comes to Me shall never hunger, and he who believes in Me shall never thirst" (John 6:35).

Dave Hunt comments that if the Calvinist understanding were true, then the rebuke the Lord Jesus issued
was "an unjust accusation to level at those who *could not*
come unless God caused them to do so."[3]

Remember, too, that according to Calvinism, regeneration precedes faith and faith is a gift. So if a person is
not elect, then he never will be regenerated, and he will
never be given the gift of faith.

George Bryson says concerning the unwillingness of
the listeners:

> Here our Lord specifically tells us why these
> men did not have the Father's Word abiding in
> them. It was not because they were not elect
> or that they were not irresistibly or effectually
> called. It was not because they had not been
> subjected to irresistible grace. It was because
> they inexcusably did not believe in God's Son.
> Here our Lord tells us why they could not have
> eternal life. It was not for any of the reasons
> Calvinism suggests. Rather it was because they
> were not willing to come to God's Son in faith.[4]

The Lord Jesus here did not speak of faith as a gift
He gives. Quite the opposite. He chided His listeners
for their culpable unwillingness to come to Him in faith
"*that you may have life.*" Clearly the Lord was saying
that faith precedes regeneration, i.e., one must believe in
Jesus *so that he might have life.*

---

[3] Dave Hunt, *What Love Is This? Calvinism's Misrepresentation of God*,
Second Edition (Bend, OR: The Berean Call, 2004), 118, emphasis his.
[4] George Bryson, *The Dark Side of Calvinism* (Santa Ana, CA: Calvary
Chapel Publishing, 2004), 202-203.

Hodges's commentary is very helpful at this point:

> Their failure to find Jesus as the Christ in the testimony of God's word was due to a fundamental unwillingness "**to come to** [Him] **that** [they] **might have life**." Very simply put, they do not believe in Him because they do not want to believe in Him. They "**are not willing**" (*ou thelete*) to allow the Scriptures to lead them to God's Son. Their searching of the Scriptures would never bring them to Jesus, of course, if they were not open to the Scriptural witness. They refuse, therefore, to hear the voice of His Father in their own Bible![5]

Contrasting the Legalistic Jews of John 5:39-40 and the Berean Jews of Acts 17:11

The expression *searching the Scriptures* is only found twice in the New Testament: John 5:39 and Acts 17:11. Both refer to Jews who searched the Old Testament Scriptures (the only Scriptures existing during the ministry of Jesus and the early ministry of the Apostles).

> When they [Paul and Silas] arrived, they went into the synagogue of the Jews. These were more fair-minded than those in Thessalonica, in that they received the word with all readiness, and searched the Scriptures daily to find out whether these things were so (Acts 17:10b-11).

---

[5] Hodges, *Faith in His Name*, 116-17, emphases his.

The Jews of John 5 did not receive the word with all readiness. They were unwilling to come to Jesus that they might have life. Here was the long-promised Messiah, reaching out to them and offering them the free gift of everlasting life. And they were not willing to receive it. They were close-minded. They had read the Old Testament many times, and they were convinced that good Jews like themselves would get into the kingdom. They knew the Old Testament commands and felt they kept them well enough to get into the coming kingdom. They didn't need Jesus. They considered Him to be an imposter. He wasn't teaching works salvation. Therefore, they rejected Him with no prayer and no additional searching of the Scriptures to see if what He was saying might be so.

The Jews of Berea were polar opposites. They, too, were probably shocked at the teaching of Paul and Silas. This justification by faith apart from the works of the Law teaching probably offended them. The idea that Messiah had to die and rise again was new to them. But instead of being unwilling to come to Jesus, they received the word with all readiness to believe. They searched the Scriptures to see if what Paul and Silas said was true. The result was, "Therefore, many of them believed, and also not a few of the Greeks, prominent women as well as men" (Acts 17:12).

They believed because they received the word with all readiness and searched the Scriptures. That is what the word *therefore* is telling us in Acts 17:12. By contrast, the Jews of John 5:39-40 did not believe because they were unwilling to do what the Jews of Berea were willing to do.

Comparing the two texts shows that searching the Bible is only effective if the one doing the searching is open to the truth. Is he willing to come to Jesus that he may have life? Both the Old Testament and New Testament teach that Jesus gives everlasting life to those who believe in Him, yet most of the Jews of the first century rejected that teaching. So do most people who call themselves *Christians* today.

Are you willing to come to Jesus? Are you open to the truth? Calvinists don't think that is important or even possible. But the Lord and His Apostles surely thought it was both.

John 5:39-40 Contradicts Unconditional Election

No Calvinist would say today what the Lord Jesus said in John 5:39-40 because it contradicts Calvinism.

The issue of willingness or unwillingness is a non-issue according to Calvinism. The only thing that matters is whether one has been elected by God. If so, then he will be regenerated and then given faith in Christ as a gift.

But that was not what the Lord Jesus taught. He taught that unbelievers were capable of believing in Him. He taught that the issue was willingness or unwillingness.

Is Calvinism Biblical? No. John 5:39-40 shows that Calvinism is inconsistent with Scripture.

SECTION 3

Limited Atonement

CHAPTER 5

Christic *Christ Took Away the Sins of the Whole World (John 1:29)*

> The next day John saw Jesus coming toward him, and said, "Behold! The Lamb of God who takes away the sin of the world!"

DID THE LORD JESUS DIE for your sins when He shed His blood on the cross? He did if He died for the sins *of the whole world.*

However, if he only died for the sins *of a small select group*, then the odds are very good that He did not die for *you.* And if He didn't die for everyone's sins, you can't know where you will spend eternity until after you have died. Only then will you will find out if you are one of the elect Christ died for.[1]

---

[1] This uncertainty is highlighted by the way that some people have claimed special revelation that Jesus has died for them.

And when you talk to your children about the Lord Jesus Christ and His death on the cross, you can't say, "Jesus died on the cross for *your* sins."

Limited Atonement Explained

Limited atonement is closely connected with *unconditional election*. According to Calvinism, Christ died only for that small group of people whom God elected for everlasting life.

Calvinists believe it is vital to recognize that Christ did not die for everyone. That is a key part of the good news (so-called).

Non-Calvinists scratch their heads at that thought.

Let's say that by the end of this age there will have been 20 billion people on earth. According to Calvinism, Christ died for say 1-2 billion of those people. Those people will spend eternity in the kingdom. The rest will spend eternity in the lake of fire because they weren't elected and Christ did not die for them.

How is it good news that Christ only died for one in ten of your family, friends, and neighbors? Isn't that bad news?

The people who will go to the lake of fire never had a chance. Since Christ did not die for them, there was no way they could ever be born again. Everlasting life is only for those for whom Christ died.

Calvinists say this is fair because we chose to sin in Adam, our forefather. In this view, when Adam sinned, he guaranteed that most of humanity would have no opportunity to be born again. If that doesn't seem fair to you,[2] they say you have a wrong view of fairness.

John 1:29 Contradicts Limited Atonement

Here is what John the Baptist said in John 1:29: "The next day John saw Jesus coming toward him, and said, 'Behold! The Lamb of God who takes away the sin of the world!'"

In order to understand what this means, let's consider the meaning of the words *world* (*kosmos*) and *takes away* (*airō*).

The World (Kosmos)

The word *kosmos* is used more in John (78 times) than any other book in the New Testament. It is used in the following ways (with some overlap between the categories):

Planet earth (where we live)

John 17:11, "I am no longer in the world, but these are in the world…"

John 17:18b, "I also have sent them into the world."

---

[2] Another view of Rom 5:12-21 is that Paul was saying that "death spread to all men, because all sinned" (Rom 5:12) refers to the sin nature which is passed from father to his children. All children descended from Adam, that is, all of us, *personally sin*. In this view we are not guilty of the death penalty due to Adam's sin being imputed to us, but due to our own sin. His sin resulted in our being enslaved to sin. But we will not be condemned because of Adam's sin. Indeed, we won't even be condemned for our own sin, since Christ died for our sins. Condemnation is for those who do not believe in Jesus (e.g., John 3:18). See notes 3-5 below.

The unbelieving system of thought

> John 7:7, "The world...hates Me because I testify of it, that its works are evil."

> John 15:19b, "If you were of the world, the world would love its own."

The present age

> John 12:31, "Now is the judgment of this world; now the ruler of this world will be cast out."

> John 16:11, "the ruler of this world is judged."

All humans of all time

> John 1:9, "That was the true Light which gives light to every man coming into the world."

> John 3:16, "For God so loved the world that He gave His only begotten Son..."

> John 3:19, "...the light has come into the world..."

> John 9:5, "As long as I am in the world, I am the light of the world."

> John 11:27, "I believe that You are the Christ, the Son of God, who is to come into the world."

The last use is the most prevalent. In John's Gospel, most of the time *kosmos* refers to all humans of all time.

When John the Baptist said that Jesus is "the Lamb of God, who takes away the sin of the world," he was not talking about the sins of the planet, or of a system of thought, or of the present age. He was saying that

Jesus fulfills the Old Testament sacrificial system and takes away the sins of all humans of all time.

Calvinists wish to define *world* as the people whom God elected. Yet there is not a single verse anywhere which identifies *the world* with those who have been chosen (for everlasting life or for anything for that matter). They are forced to adopt a meaning for *kosmos* which fits their theology, not the Scriptures.

Roger Olson says,

> Let's look again at John 3:16. Everybody knows it by heart. It says God loves the "world." Calvinists either do not believe that refers to everybody without exception, or they say (with John Piper) that God loves even the nonelect in some ways. Both explanations of John 3:16 fail to make sense. The best critical exegetes of John 3:16 affirm it does mean "the whole human race." Even some Calvinists cannot agree with their fellow Calvinists that in that passage "world" refers only to the elect. They recognize all too well what the interpretation that limits "world" to only some people from every tribe and nation would do to other verses that mention "world" in John's gospel.[3]

David Allen agrees, saying, "No linguistic, exegetical, or theological grounds exist for reducing the meaning of 'world' to 'the elect.'"[4]

---

[3] Roger E. Olson, *Against Calvinism* (Grand Rapids, MI: Zondervan, 2011), 134.
[4] David L. Allen and Steve W. Lemke, *Whosoever Will: A Biblical-Theological Critique of Five-Point Calvinism* (Nashville, TN: B & H Academic, 2010), 80.

So, too, Leroy Forlines, commenting on John 3:16, argues,

> The only way anyone would ever question that "world" in this verse meant anything other than every human being is that he comes to the verse with a theological conviction that will not allow him to believe that. In this case the burden of proof is on the person who wants to place a restriction upon the scope of the word "world."[5]

Takes Away (Airō)

This word is used often in John (26 times). In most cases it refers to something physical which is taken or taken away. Jesus told those at the tomb of Lazarus to *take away* the stone (John 11:39). When the women got to Jesus' tomb, they found that the stone had been *taken away* (John 20:1).The women reported to the disciples, "They have *taken away* the Lord out of the tomb" (John 20:2). Jesus told the man whom He healed, "Rise, *take up* your bed and walk" (John 5:8).

John 1:29 refers to the taking away of something intangible, i.e., the sins of the *kosmos*. Some have mistakenly thought that this refers to forgiveness. Yet *airō* is not a word that refers to forgiveness in the New Testament.

Every person has a load of sins. Unless God had done something to deal with our sins, no one could be born again because our sins block us from God's life. But that is where the death of Christ comes in. When

---

[5] F. Leroy Forlines, *The Quest for Truth* (Nashville, TN: Randall House, 2001), 406.

Jesus died on the cross, He took away that load of sin that barred us from God. This taking away of sin is the removal of sin as a barrier between God and man.[6] Many gospel tracts show the cross of Jesus spanning the gap between perfect God and sinful man.[7] Such tracts are teaching unlimited atonement.

With sins taken away, the issue for the sinner is not how to deal with his own sins, but whether or not he will believe in the Savior who took them away.

After quoting John 1:29 and other texts, Laurence Vance says, "Beginning with the Gospel of John, it is clear that the Lamb of God took away the sin of the world. Or did he?"[8] He then goes on to quote Pink, Gunn, Owen, Hoeksema, and other Calvinists who "have worked overtime to nullify" verses like John 3:16 and John 1:29.

---

[6] Some suggest that John 1:29 means that the Lord Jesus *potentially* took away the sins of the world, but that He *actually* only does so when a person believes in Him. That is not what John the Baptist said. The verb means *to take away*, not *to potentially take away*. The rock was taken away from the tomb of Lazarus. It was not *potentially* taken away. Unlimited atonement teaches that everyone is capable of being born again if he simply believes in the Lord Jesus Christ for everlasting life.

[7] See, for example, *How to Have a Happy and Meaningful Life (DTS)*, *The Best News You'll Ever Hear* (Bryant and Hodges), *Steps to Peace with God* (Billy Graham), and *The Four Spiritual Laws* (Cru). While these tracts give different conditions on what one must do to have everlasting life, they all teach unlimited atonement.

[8] Laurence M. Vance, *The Other Side of Calvinism*, Revised Edition (Pensacola, FL: Vance Publications, 1991, 1999), 434.

The Calvinist Explanation of John 1:29
Doesn't Make Sense

Calvinism argues that *kosmos* in John 1:29 refers to the elect. If so, why didn't John the Baptist say that? He could have said, "Behold, the Lamb of God who takes away the sin of the elect."

They must make the same argument concerning John 3:16, "For God so loved *the elect* that He gave His only begotten Son…" But the Lord didn't say that. He said the Father so loved *the world*. And no other meaning of *world* fits in John 3:16 (or 1:29). God didn't love this present age. Nor did He love the world system that opposes God. Nor did He send Jesus to die for the planet. He loved all the people of this planet and of this age.

Even more bizarre is the Calvinist explanation of 1 John 2:2, "And He Himself is the propitiation for our sins, and not for ours only but also for the whole world." Calvinists are forced to say that Jesus satisfied the sins *for the elect in Asia Minor*, and not only the elect there, but also for *the whole world of the elect*.

Of course, the most natural reading of all these texts is that *kosmos* refers to all of humanity, all who have lived, all who live now, and all who will live in the future until the end of the Millennium.

Limited Atonement Minimizes Christ's Death

By His death on the cross, the Lord Jesus removed the sin barrier between man and God, and made it possible for *everyone* to be born again by faith in Him. The Calvinist idea that Jesus only died for a small percentage of humanity trivializes the death of Christ.

According to Calvinism, Christ did not die for the vast majority of people.[9] Thus most people were doomed from conception. The death of Christ is not for them. It has no value for them. They cannot be born again.

Since, according to the tenets of Calvinism, Christ did not die for most people, most people are doomed to eternal condemnation. Indeed, they were doomed before time began and will be tormented forever no matter what.

To Calvinists that seems Biblical and fair. But to those of us who simply read the Bible and derive our beliefs from it, that seems to be a direct contradiction to the Word of God. It also seems to contradict the fact that God is just. Nothing God does is unjust.

Jesus is the Lamb of God who took away the sins of the world. John 1:29 demonstrates that Calvinism is not in agreement with the Word of God.

---

[9] Calvinists suggest that if Christ had died for everyone, then everyone would end up in the kingdom and no one would be condemned. Calvinists think that Christ would never die for someone unless He was going to give that person everlasting life. But that is not true. The Bible clearly states that Jesus died for the sins of the whole world. And it says that most will be eternally condemned (Matt 7:13-14; Rev 20:11-15). Both are true. The fact that Christ removed sin as a barrier does not mean that everyone has everlasting life. It means that all are capable of having everlasting life. But to get that life, one must believe in Jesus, as He repeatedly said (e.g., John 5:39-40).

CHAPTER 6

False Teachers Bought by the Lord (2 Peter 2:1)

ACCORDING TO THE THIRD POINT of Calvinism (limited atonement), Christ died only for the elect when He died on the cross. That is, He paid the price of redemption only for the small percentage of humanity whom God (supposedly) unconditionally chose before time began.

Such a view may seem to make sense. After all, Calvinists will say that God succeeds in all He does. Thus if the death of Christ is designed to produce salvation, then it will produce salvation for 100% of the people for whom He died, without exception. The problem with this view is that it is not taught in Scripture. Worse still, that view is actually contrary to Scripture. Second Peter 2:1 is one such text which contradicts the Calvinist view.

If it can be shown from Scripture that Christ died for even one person who will spend eternity in the lake of fire, then limited atonement is clearly false.

Peter was writing prophetically in the second chapter of his second epistle. He said, "there will be false teachers among you, who will secretly bring in destructive heresies…" Jude, written slightly after 2 Peter, reported that the false teachers had now come on the scene (Jude 12-19).

These False Teachers Were Unregenerate

Nearly all commentators agree that these false teachers were unregenerate.[1] Of course some people wrongly think that all false teachers are unregenerate. They reason that God will not allow a regenerate person to fall into and teach false doctrine. But the Scriptures actually warn believers of this possibility. Paul wrote Timothy about born-again people who were teaching false doctrine and upsetting the faith of some (1 Tim 1:18-20; 2 Tim 2:16-18). He even publicly rebuked the Apostles Peter and Barnabas, for failing to be straightforward about the truth of the gospel (Gal 2:11-21).

That the false teachers of 2 Peter 2 are not regenerate is evident by what Peter says in 2 Pet 2:17:

> These are wells without water, clouds carried by a tempest, *for whom is reserved the blackness of darkness forever* (emphasis added).

---

[1] See, for example, J. N. D. Kelly, *A Commentary on the Epistles of Peter and Jude* (Grand Rapids, MI: Baker: 1969), 345; Michael Green, *The Second Epistle of Peter and the Epistle of Jude* (Grand Rapids, MI: Eerdmans, 1968), 115; Kenneth O. Gangel, *2 Peter* in *The Bible Knowledge Commentary,* NT Edition, eds. John F. Walvoord and Roy B. Zuck (NP: Scripture Press, 1983), 873.

The kingdom of God is a kingdom of everlasting light, not of everlasting darkness (John 8:12; 12:35; Acts 26:18; Rom 13:12; 2 Cor 6:14; 1 Pet 2:9; 1 John 1:5; Rev 21:23).

Christ Bought These Unregenerate False Teachers

Of these soon-to-appear false teachers, Peter said that they "will secretly bring in destructive heresies, *even denying the Lord who bought them*, and bring on themselves swift destruction" (2 Pet 2:1, emphasis added).

The word translated *bought* is *agorazō*. The word is used in the Gospels to refer to buying food, fields, animals, oil, linen, and so forth (Matt 13:44, 46; 14:15; 25:9; Mark 6:37; 15:46; Luke 14:19; John 4:8; 13:29). In 1 Corinthians and the book of Revelation it is used to refer to buying, or redeeming, people by the blood of Christ:

> 1 Cor 6:20, "For *you were bought* with a price…"
>
> 1 Cor 7:23, "*You were bought* with a price…"
>
> Rev 5:9, "And they sang a new song, saying: "*You…have redeemed* us to God by Your blood…"
>
> Rev 14:3, "the hundred and forty-four thousand *who were redeemed* from the earth."
>
> Rev 14:4, "*These were redeemed* from among men…"

Peter also spoke of redemption in his first epistle. Though he used a different Greek word, *lutroō*, he was speaking of the exact same redemption found in 2 Pet 2:1: "you were not *redeemed* with corruptible things, like silver or gold…but *with the precious blood of Christ*, as a lamb without blemish and without spot" (emphasis added).

Laurence Vance discusses two ways in which Calvinists attempt to explain 2 Pet 2:1: they suggest that "the Lord" refers to God the Father, not Jesus, and they suggest that "bought" does not mean "bought."[2] Vance concludes the text is clear that Jesus indeed bought false teachers, men bound for the lake of fire.

If Christ Bought People Who Will End Up in the Lake of Fire, Then the Atonement Is Unlimited

All of the references cited above from 1 Corinthians and Revelation and 1 Peter refer to born-again people who were bought by the blood of Christ.

The fact that Christ died for the Church does not mean that He did not die for everyone. In his book *Christian Theology* Millard Erickson comments:

> To be sure, there are also those texts that speak of Christ's dying for his sheep and for the church. These texts, however, present no problem if we regard the universal passages as normative or determinative. Certainly if Christ died for the whole, there is no problem in asserting that he died for a specific part of the whole. To insist that those passages which focus on his dying for his people require the understanding that he died only for them and not for any others contradicts the universal passages. We conclude that the hypothesis of universal

[2] Laurence M. Vance, *The Other Side of Calvinism*, Revised Edition (Pensacola, FL: Vance Publications, 1991, 1999), 456-57.

atonement is able to account for a larger seg-
ment of the biblical witness with less distortion
than is the hypothesis of limited atonement.[3]

The fact that Peter says that the coming false teachers also have been bought by Christ (2 Pet 2:1) shows
that the atonement was for everyone, not simply a small
portion of humanity. After citing 1 Tim 4:10, 1 John 2:2,
and Isa 53:6, texts showing the universality of Christ's
atoning work, texts which he says, "cannot be ignored,"
Erickson adds, "We must also consider statements like
2 Peter 2:1, which affirms that some for whom Christ
died do perish."[4] A bit earlier he had said, "2 Peter 2:1
seems to point out most clearly that people for whom
Christ died may be lost."[5]

Robert Picirilli concurs:

> The Calvinist explanation of 2 Peter 2:1 is
> another example of reading into the sentence
> something manifestly not implied. These words
> too are straightforward: The Lord Jesus, by His
> death, bought them. They deny Him. Nothing
> else is justified by the text.[6]

Picirilli goes on to point out that Peter does not say
that the coming false teachers *professed* to be Christians,

[3] Millard Erickson, *Christian Theology*, Second Edition (Grand Rapids,
MI: Baker Academics, 1983, 1984, 1985, 1998), 851.

[4] Ibid.

[5] Ibid., 847.

[6] Robert E. Picirilli, *Grace, Faith, Free Will: Contrasting Views of Salvation: Calvinism & Arminianism* (Nashville, TN: Randall House, 2002),
114.

or that they were *professing* that Christ bought them. Rather, *Peter says that Jesus bought them.*[7]

Even Calvin Probably Believed in Unlimited Atonement

Calvinism is a somewhat misleading term. Most people think that Calvinism is what Calvin taught. Actually, it is what later followers of Calvin taught.

I am not a Calvin scholar. People devote their lives to studying Calvin's writings. I have not. So I will not attempt to give quotes from the *Institutes* (or his commentaries) to prove my point here. But I will pass on what a Calvin scholar has said.

At an annual meeting of the Evangelical Theological Society (ETS), a Calvin scholar delivered a paper addressing whether Calvin taught limited or unlimited atonement. I listened with great interest to his message. He gave a series of quotes from Calvin's *Institutes* showing that Calvin seemed to indicate that he taught limited atonement. He gave another group of quotes from the *Institutes* showing that Calvin clearly taught unlimited atonement. The speaker indicated that in the *Institutes* there were more references to unlimited atonement than to limited atonement. And the statements about unlimited atonement were unambiguous. Thus he concluded that while we should not be dogmatic in this regard, it appears that Calvin believed in unlimited atonement.

Of course, what matters is what the Scriptures teach, not what Calvin taught. However, it is enlightening to

---

[7] Ibid.

me that there is plenty of evidence in Calvin's own writings that he held to unlimited atonement.

Evangelism Is Richer Since
Unlimited Atonement Is True

The Calvinist cannot say to someone, "The good news is that Christ died on the cross *for your sins.*" That is because Calvinists believe that Christ only died for the sins of about 10% (or less) of humanity. The other 90+% are helpless, hopeless, and hell-bound. Jesus will never be their Savior and Redeemer. The Lord did not buy them.

That is *not* what the Word of God teaches.

Christ died for *all*, even for false teachers who will spend eternity in the realm of darkness forever. Because that is true, we can indeed tell people, "The good news is that Christ died on the cross *for your sins*. He has made you savable. You don't need to take care of your own sins. He already took away your sins (John 1:29). Thus, your transgressions no longer bar you from everlasting life. If you simply believe in Him, you will pass from death into life (John 5:24)."

People do not need to pay for their own sins. Nor could they. Christ paid for all the sins of the children of Adam. He *finished* the work of redemption on the cross ("It is finished!" John 19:30). Now all anyone needs to do is believe in the Lord Jesus, and he will have everlasting life that can never be lost. That is indeed good news.

Second Peter 2:1 contradicts Calvinism.

SECTION 4

Irresistible Grace

CHAPTER 7

God Is Drawing All, Not Just a Few (John 12:32)

"And I, if I am lifted up from the earth, will draw all *peoples* to Myself."

THE IDEA OF *IRRESISTIBLE GRACE* (the I in TULIP) is that anyone God is drawing to Himself will be born again and then will come to faith in Christ (in that order). God's drawing cannot be resisted. Once again, this is based on the view that whatever God does, He succeeds in. Therefore, if He draws someone to Himself so that the person might be born again, that person will be born again and will come to faith. Thus if the way is narrow that leads to life and few find it, only few are being drawn.

This doctrine is viewed by Calvinists as a fantastic thing. They understand irresistible grace to mean that the elect cannot possibly fail to be born again and to persevere (the fifth point). God draws 100% of the elect. And all who are drawn by God's grace will be born again and will persevere.

What about those who are not being drawn? Practically speaking, irresistible grace means that nine out of ten (or 99 out of 100) of your relatives (children, brothers and sisters, aunts and uncles, parents, grandparents, grandchildren, etc.) will never be drawn by God and are doomed to eternal condemnation. There is no hope for those not being drawn. For them, and for most people, election and irresistible grace are not good news at all, but bad news.

Witnessing to most of your relatives, neighbors, friends, and coworkers is guaranteed to be ineffective since most of them are not being drawn and thus are incapable of coming to faith in Christ.

While the fourth point might at least seem comforting for Calvinists, it is not. The problem is that Calvinism teaches that Calvinists may *think* they have been irresistibly drawn, when in fact they have not been. Many people profess faith in Christ. But, according to Calvinism, a large percentage of those who profess faith—even a large percentage of Calvinists!—are people who only *think* that they were drawn and chosen and were beneficiaries of Christ's death.

Calvinism teaches that false professors attend Calvinist churches, get baptized, give money, and even serve as pastors, elders, deacons, and Bible study leaders. Many if not most of them will be sincere. They will look like born-again people. But if they were not actually drawn by God, then their profession will be shown to be false because they will not persevere (the fifth point), and they will spend eternity in the lake of fire, separated from the Lord Jesus and His kingdom.

If irresistible grace is true, then no one, not even a Calvinist pastor or theologian, can be sure that he has been drawn and elected and redeemed by God. Only persevering until death can show that. Thus according to Calvinism's fourth point, only time will tell whether one has truly been irresistibly drawn to God's grace by the Holy Spirit. After you die, you will find out where you are going. Before then, you can't be sure.

John 12:32 Shows That God Draws All

The word *draw* (*helkuō*) occurs only five times in John. Three refer to literal drawing. One use refers to *drawing a sword* (John 18:10) and two to *drawing fish* in a net, to a boat, and to land (John 21:6, 11). However, notice an important difference in the last two literal uses. Whereas John 21:6 refers to *ineffective* efforts to draw fish into a boat, John 21:11 refers to *effective* efforts to draw those same fish to shore.

Only two of the five uses are figurative. These two refer to God drawing (attracting, wooing) people to Himself. The leading dictionary of the New Testament says of those two uses, "to draw a person in the direction of values for inner life, *draw, attract*" (BDAG, p. 318).

One of those uses is John 12:32, which reads, "And I, if I am lifted up from the earth, will draw all *peoples* to Myself." John then adds this comment, "This He said, signifying by what death He would die" (John 12:33).

The word *peoples* is supplied by the translators. A more literal translation would be, "I…will draw all to Myself." Jesus was promising to draw all to Himself. Not

1% or 5% or 10%. All. However, while Jesus draws all, He does not indicate that everyone will come to faith in Him. Drawing makes faith in Christ *possible*, but not *inevitable* (cf. Matt 7:13-14; 23:37-39).

But how does John's comment about the cross (i.e., about Jesus being lifted up) relate to drawing?

One view is that the Lord meant that if He was going to die on the cross for the sins of the world, He would follow that up by also attracting all to Himself. The Lord would not lay down His life for us without also taking pains to then woo us to Him so that we might believe in Him and be born again.

Another possibility is that the cross in itself is a drawing of all men to the Lord Jesus Christ. Jesus' death on the cross is one of the most well known events in all of history. That event pictures the love of God (John 3:16) and attracts people, draws people, toward faith in Christ.

Anthony Badger takes the second view concerning John 12:32:

> People who are drawn to the Savior are those who hear of Jesus, His perfect sinless life, His unjust (humanly speaking) substitutionary death, His bodily resurrection from the dead, His bodily ascension into Heaven, the promise of His glorious return, etc. The gospel message about Jesus draws folks to Him and the gospel offer to believe in Him for freely given eternal life clinches the matter for those who are

convinced and fully assured He will keep His promise."[1]

Leroy Forlines takes that view as well. He says,

> When we go to John 12:32, the natural meaning of the verse is to understand *helkuō* in terms of *influence* and *response* rather than *cause* and *effect*…Jesus…definitely did not mean that He would drag every human being to Himself. He meant that there would go out from Him a drawing power that would make it possible for any person who hears the gospel to come to Him.[2]

The latter view fits the context better (see also John 1:9; 3:14-16).

However, in light of John 16:7-11, the former is true as well. The Holy Spirit draws all people to Christ.

If you wish, you can move on to Chapter 8. The point is clear. John 12:32 is a showstopper for Calvinism.

However, if you want more evidence, read on. Two other passages in John's Gospel confirm what we've already concluded about John 12:32. We will now consider John 16:7-11 and John 6:44.

John 16:7-11 Says God Convicts All

In Jesus' final discourse He spoke about what the Holy Spirit would do after He ascended to heaven:

---

[1] Anthony B. Badger, *Confronting Calvinism* (Columbia, SC: NP, 2013), 78.

[2] F. Leroy Forlines, *The Quest for Truth* (Nashville, TN: Randall House, 2001), 386, emphases his.

> Nevertheless I tell you the truth. It is to your
> advantage that I go away; for if I do not go away,
> the Helper will not come to you; but if I depart,
> I will send Him to you. And when He has come,
> He will convict the world of sin, and of righ-
> teousness, and of judgment: of sin, because they
> do not believe in Me; of righteousness, because
> I go to My Father and you see Me no more; of
> judgment, because the ruler of this world is
> judged.

While those verses do not use the word *drawing*, clearly *conviction* is a synonym. The Holy Spirit convicts *the world* of three things: our sin, Jesus' righteousness, and coming judgment.

BDAG says that this convicting (Greek *elenchō*) means "to bring a person to the point of recognizing wrongdoing, *convict, convince* someone of something, point something out to someone" (p. 315). The Spirit convinces or points out to people their sinfulness, God's righteousness, and coming judgment after this life is over. All of this is part of God's drawing or attracting people to the Lord Jesus Christ.

While the Lord did not say why the Holy Spirit does this, the eleven surely understood this to mean that their witness would be preceded by the work of the Spirit. When they would talk with someone about Jesus, the Holy Spirit would have already convicted him of the fact that he is a sinner, that God is righteous, and that there is a coming judgment.

It is not just Christianity that teaches that there will be a coming judgment. The world's religions teach that there is a coming judgment. They also teach that we are sinners and that God is righteous. Might it be due to the work of the Spirit that nearly all religions teach these three truths?

The purpose of this conviction is to move people to believe in Jesus for everlasting life. People know they are sinners and that God is righteous and that there is a coming judgment. They need a way of escape. Jesus is the way. He is the only way.

The Spirit convicts *the world*, all of humanity.

How does He do this? Certainly the Holy Spirit uses believers to convict people via evangelism, teaching, and preaching.

The Holy Spirit uses nature to convict people (Ps 19:1; Rom 1:18-32). He also uses our consciences to convict us (Rom 2:15).

In addition, He can even use the words of unbelievers to convict people. People who go to works-salvation churches will be convicted about their sinfulness, about God's righteousness, and about coming judgment. While the solution given in such churches—commit your life to Christ, obey Him, and persevere in obedience till death—is ineffective, people nonetheless can see their need clearly.

I was in a works-salvation cult for 14 years, from ages 6 to 20. While I was hopelessly confused, I did know I was a sinner, God is righteous, and judgment is coming. I was convicted. When the Holy Spirit then had a friend challenge my view of the gospel and invite me to an evangelistic meeting, I was open enough to go (praying for God to protect me from false teaching). The conviction led to me hearing and believing the promise of life.

John 6:44 Does Not Say Only Some Are Drawn

Calvinists don't refer much to John 12:32. Possibly that is because it is such a difficult verse for their position. However, if there are only two figurative uses of *drawing* in John's Gospel, we must study both of them to get a good idea about what the Lord meant. To ignore one of them is a mistake.[3]

In his commentary on John, J. Ramsey Michaels says, "The apparent universal scope of 'all' is striking."[4] Though he goes on to suggest that those being drawn are "a specific group,"[5] he does not identify that group as the elect. Instead he says the group is "those who actually 'come' to Jesus in faith, for salvation."[6] That explanation does not fit with the Calvinist framework. And it can be argued that Michaels's initial statement is true. The text says that. The scope of God's drawing is indeed universal.

An anonymous blogger suggests that the drawing is indeed of all, "When we consider Jn. 12:32 and Jn. 6:44 together, we are justified to conclude, with Kittle, that the drawing spoken of in these passages has reference to a universal, and therefore resistible, drawing."[7]

---

[3] Because we understand difficult passages in light of the simpler passages, the need to study John 12:32 along with and even before John 6:44 is even more pressing. To bypass John 12:32, or to attempt to explain it away because one has a preconceived understanding of John 6:44, is the opposite of good hermeneutics.

[4] J. Ramsey Michaels, *The Gospel of John*, NICNT (Grand Rapids, MI: Eerdmans, 2010), 698.

[5] Ibid., 699.

[6] Ibid.

[7] https://arminianperspectives.wordpress.com/category/john-1232/. Accessed August 19, 2017.

Calvinists do refer frequently to the only other figurative use of *drawing* in the fourth Gospel, John 6:44. There the Lord said,

> "No one can come to Me unless the Father who sent Me draws him; and I will raise him up at the last day."

Calvinists think that the Lord was saying something like this: *The Father is drawing only a small portion of humanity to Me, and all of those select few whom He draws will come to Me.*

But that is not at all what the Lord said. That is reading one's theology into a text, trying to make it say what it does not say so that you have somewhere to hang your doctrinal hat.

While Calvinists often refer to John 6:44, they don't really pay sufficient attention to what it is actually saying.

In John's Gospel *coming to Jesus* refers to believing in Him (see John 5:39-40; 6:35). That is surely the case here. So we might paraphrase John 6:44 in this way: *No one can believe in Me unless the Father who sent Me draws him to Me…*

What percentage of those whom the Father draws to Jesus come to faith in Him? The Lord Jesus does not say. Calvinists *assume* that 100% of those drawn come to faith. *But Jesus didn't say that here or anywhere else.* And what Jesus said elsewhere actually contradicts that conclusion. Note what the Lord Jesus said one chapter earlier, in John 5:39-40, in a context that is directly dealing with everlasting life:

> "You search the Scriptures, for in them you think you have eternal life; and these are they

> which testify of Me. But you are not willing to come to Me that you may have life."

It is hard to imagine any people in all of human history being more drawn to Jesus than those living in Israel in Jesus' day. They either personally saw or heard eyewitness reports that He raised the dead, gave sight to the blind, healed paralytics, cast out demons, restored withered hands, walked on water, fed 5,000 men with one boy's lunch, and taught in a way that astounded even the experts in Jewish law. He was accessible for three and a half years of public ministry. What He said on the cross was unlike what anyone ever said who approached death. When He yielded up His spirit in death, the veil in the temple was torn from top to bottom, an earthquake occurred, and many Old Testament saints who had been buried were raised from the dead and came out of their tombs and walked among the people (Matt 27:51-53). For forty days Jesus appeared repeatedly to up to 500 people (1 Cor 15:5-11). You think the Jews in Israel during Jesus' ministry were being drawn to Him? Of course they were. Yet most of His own people to whom Jesus ministered did not believe in Him as John 1:11 sadly reports.

They were not willing to come to Jesus. Just as in John 6:44, the issue in John 1:11-12 and 5:39-40 is coming to Jesus. And the determining factor is not the Father's drawing, but personal willingness to believe in Him.

Based on John 12:32 (and John 5:39-40; 16:7-11), the percentage the Father draws to Jesus is 100%. He draws all. Those who are willing to come to Jesus do so. The ones unwilling do not.

Jesus' point is that 0% come to Him without the Father's drawing. But since the Father is drawing all, that makes it possible for anyone and everyone to come to faith in Christ. But it does not mean they all will. We know from Jesus' teaching elsewhere that few will come to faith in Him (Matt 7:13-14).

Notice this statement by Paul and Barnabas concerning Jews who actively rejected their preaching about the Lord Jesus Christ:

> "It was necessary that the word of God should be spoken to you first; but *since you reject it, and judge yourselves unworthy of everlasting life,* behold, we turn to the Gentiles" (Acts 13:46, emphasis added).

Conclusion

John 12:32 refutes Calvinism. Contrary to Calvinism, the Lord Jesus is drawing *all* to Himself. Those who are willing to come to faith in Jesus will believe in Him. Those who are not will not.

The Lord Jesus paid for all the sins of every person who will ever live. He shed His blood for everyone's past, present, and future sins. He paid it all and left us nothing to pay.

But He went further. He not only made salvation possible, He woos everyone to Himself. He wants all to believe in Him. He is attracting us to Him via the ministry of the Holy Spirit in the world.

Don't draw the wrong conclusion. If you think God is only drawing a select few, and the drawing (like the Calvinist understanding of election and saving faith) is unknowable, then you cannot be sure that you are born again. You will always wonder if God gave you life and faith (T), if He truly elected you (U), if Christ really died for you (L), if you really were being drawn (I), and if you really will persevere to the end of your life (P).

God is drawing everyone. Therefore everyone is a candidate for everlasting life. Though most will not come to faith (Matt 7:13-14), the door is open to all. God is not arbitrarily wooing only a select few. He is drawing all toward the Lord Jesus Christ. Those who are willing to believe in Jesus will believe and will have everlasting life.

CHAPTER 8

Unbelieving Israel Resisted God's Grace (Matthew 23:37-39)

THE FOURTH POINT OF CALVINISM is *irresistible grace.* Calvinists say that God's favor cannot be resisted because God accomplishes all that He wishes to be accomplished. So if He wants to pour His favor on someone by electing him to eternal salvation, He does so, and man cannot resist God.

While that may sound logical, it is only logical if God has determined that all which He wishes to do He accomplishes. If God determined that men have the ability to resist His will, then men have that ability. The sovereign God is capable of allowing men to resist Him. The question is, what do the Scriptures say? Do the Scriptures give any examples of anyone ever resisting God?

Matthew 23:37-39 is an irrefutable example of men who resisted God's grace. It is a showstopper for Calvinism.

God Wanted to Gather Israel to Himself, But the Nation Was Unwilling

The Lord said,

> "O Jerusalem, Jerusalem, the one who kills the prophets and stones those who are sent to her! How often I wanted to gather your children together, as a hen gathers her chicks under her wings, but you were not willing!" (v 37).

The Lord was lamenting about Jerusalem's rejection of Him and His kingdom. He made it clear that He was talking about the people of Jerusalem when He said, "I wanted to gather *your children* together..." The children of Jerusalem refers to the people of the chosen city.

The Lord Jesus, under the direction of God the Father, wanted to gather the people of Jerusalem, and by extension, all of Judea and all of Israel, like a hen lovingly and safely gathers her chicks under her wings.

But He did not do what He wanted to do! Let that sink in. According to Calvinism, all that God wishes to do He does. According to Jesus, the unwillingness of the people of Jerusalem led to Him not doing what He wanted to do, that is, establishing His kingdom in the first century.

God wanted to gather Israel to Himself at that time, but His grace was resisted by the Jews of the first century. He preached to that generation. He did many miracles to prove that He is indeed the Messiah and Israel's king. But the nation was not willing.[1]

---

[1] Compare Luke 19:27, "But bring here those enemies of mine, who did not want me to reign over them, and slay them before me." The enemies of Jesus who didn't want Him to reign as King over them were identified

The problem for that generation was not that God was not drawing them. The problem was that they were not willing to respond to His drawing.

Jerusalem Was Destroyed,
Though It Could Have Been Exalted

It is evident in what the Lord said that the people of Jerusalem (*you*, plural) were not willing to be gathered to the Lord, and that as a result, the kingdom did not come for that generation. Steve Lemke accurately says, "Note also that His lament concerns the entire city of Jerusalem, not just a small number of elect within Jerusalem."[2]

In AD 70 Jerusalem and the temple were destroyed. The Jewish people were exiled until 1948. Even today the nation is not a believing nation, and Messiah has not yet returned. (And more Jews live in other countries of the world, about 16 million, than live in Israel, about 7 million.)

If Israel had responded by faith to Jesus' preaching, Jerusalem and the entire nation would have been exalted. The Lord Jesus would have established His righteous kingdom in the first century, for that generation of Jews. Their unwillingness to believe in Him led to widespread death and destruction (compare Luke 13:1-5).

---

by the Lord earlier in the parable as "his citizens [who] hated him, and sent a delegation after him, saying, 'We will not have this man to reign over us'" (Luke 19:14). "His citizens" who didn't want Him as King were unbelieving Israel. Compare also John 1:11-12.

[2] David L. Allen and Steve W. Lemke, *Whosoever Will: A Biblical-Theological Critique of Five-Point Calvinism* (Nashville, TN: B & H Academic, 2010), 120.

Israel Resisted God's Grace

The point of Matt 23:37-39 is that first century Israel rejected God's will for her. God's grace was resistible, and it was resisted.[3]

In a March 4, 2006, post, a blogger named Charles wrote,

> Matthew 23:37 declares with a clarion call the heartfelt desire of Jesus to save the inhabitants of Jerusalem. The people of Jerusalem, however, were not willing to come to Jesus. This verse annihilates the Calvinist doctrine of irresistible grace and unconditional election.[4]

Remember, if there is even one example in all of Scripture of any human who resisted God's grace, then the fourth point of Calvinism collapses. And since all the points hang together, Calvinism as a system will topple.

And this is but one example. The new nation of Israel rejected God's grace when ten of the twelve spies whom Moses sent counseled the people to turn away from the Promised Land, for the inhabitants were giants whom even God could not conquer. Their resistance contributed to forty years of wandering in the wilderness, during which everyone aged twenty and over died, except for Joshua and Caleb, the two spies who had

---

[3] Some Calvinists argue that "your children" refers literally to the children of Jerusalem, not to the adults there. It is argued that Jesus was only lamenting over the religious leaders in Jerusalem, not the whole city. That argument is specious, however. See Dave Hunt, *What Love Is This? Calvinism's Misrepresentation of God*, Second Edition (Bend, OR: The Berean Call, 2004), 461-64.

[4] http://calvinistflyswatter.blogspot.com/2006/03/james-whites-eisegesis-of-matthew-2337.html. Accessed July 15, 2017.

believed God's promise and had counseled going up and taking the land.

Israel resisted God's grace in the time of the judges as well. Israel resisted God during the time of the united kingdom. And during the time of the divided kingdom. Even after the return from exile, the people resisted God. He called them a stiff-necked people.

And it was not merely Jews living in Israel that resisted God in the Old Testament and during the ministry of Jesus. Most diaspora Jews resisted God during the preaching of the Apostles. Paul said "you judge yourselves unworthy of everlasting life" (Acts 13:46). He did not say, "God judged you unworthy of everlasting life." They judged themselves unworthy of that life by resisting the preaching of Paul and the other Apostles.

Conclusion

The Lord Jesus said,

> "O Jerusalem, Jerusalem, the one who kills the prophets and stones those who are sent to her! How often I wanted to gather your children together, as a hen gathers her chicks under her wings, but you were not willing!"

Those words contradict Calvinism. The Lord tells us that He wanted to gather Israel to Himself. He wanted to start the kingdom in the first century. He did not want Israel to reject Him, but it did. Israel rejected Him because the Jewish people "were not willing" to come to Him (John 5:39-40; see also John 7:17).

George Bryson correctly points out that the Lord could easily have said, "but you were not able."[5] The fact that the Lord said they were *not willing*, rather than *not able*, contradicts Calvinism.

Omniscience means not only knowing everything that has ever happened or ever will happen, but it also means knowing all possibilities. The Lord in His omniscience knew that if that generation of Jews had been willing to come to Him, then He would have established His kingdom then.

Matthew 23:37-39 is not consistent with the teachings of Calvinism.

---

[5] George L. Bryson, *The Five Points of Calvinism: Weighed and Found Wanting* (Costa Mesa, CA: The Word for Today, 1996), 98.

SECTION 5

Preservation of the Saints

CHAPTER 9

Preservation Even If You Fall Away (Luke 8:11-15)

CALVINISTS FORMALLY BELIEVE IN ETERNAL SECURITY, which they call *the preservation of the saints*. But practically speaking they reject that doctrine. Let me explain.

A Calvinist will say that *anyone who perseveres in faith and good works* until death will enter the kingdom, and anyone who fails to persevere will end up in the lake of fire.

Hypothetically, God might guarantee that everyone who comes to faith in Christ will persevere in faith and good works no matter what. In that case, He would determine that believers can't sin *much or for very long*.

I don't know of anyone who would not like to be guaranteed he would not fail in the Christian life. I certainly would. Yet there is no such guarantee in Scripture. And Luke 8:11-13 clearly shows that all who simply believe in the Lord Jesus Christ will be preserved forever, even if they fall away some time after coming to faith in Christ.

The Seed Is the Word of God (Luke 8:11)

The Lord specifically said that "the seed is the word of God."

Notice in this parable the repetition of the expression *the word*. It occurs in verses 11 (*the word of God*), 12 (*the word*), 13 (*the word*), and 15 (*the word*). Even verse 14 implicitly refers to the word when the Lord said, "when they have heard."

The expression *the word* refers both to the promise of life (vv 12-15) and the teaching in God's Word on discipleship (vv 14-15).

First, one must believe the word concerning everlasting life in order to have that life. Second, one must believe the word concerning discipleship in order to grow.

In order to understand this parable, or anything in God's Word, we must prayerfully observe what is written.

Observing that this parable is about people's response to the Word of God is a key first step in understanding it.

Since verse 12 speaks of the saving power of this word, this must be the word of God *concerning salvation*.

Calvinism is in a bind here. It needs to see this reference to the word of God as referring to the saving message for the first and fourth soils, but not the saving message for the second and third soils. So for the second and third soils, the Word of God does some non-saving work when it is believed, and in the fourth soil the Word of God does a saving work when it is believed.

Calvinism is forced to view the seed in soil four as being different from the seed in soils two and three. Yet the Lord indicated that the seed is the same in all four soils. If the seed in soil four is a saving seed, then it is in the first three soils as well.

Anyone Who Does Not Believe the Saving Word Is Not Saved (Luke 8:12)

The reason Satan snatches the word away is "lest they should believe and be saved." The Lord here was making a simple statement. One who believes the Word of God (concerning the saving message) is saved. One who does not believe it is not saved. Satan works to keep people from believing and being saved.

Yet Calvinism says that no one, elect or non-elect, can believe prior to the new birth. Regeneration *must* precede faith. But in Luke 8:12, the Lord said that faith precedes and results in salvation. Thus the one who does not believe is not saved.

Those on the Rocky Soil Believe the Saving Word for a Time, Then Fall Away (Luke 8:13)

This verse is fatal to the Calvinist understanding that preservation is conditioned upon perseverance. According to Calvinism, God guarantees that all who believe in Jesus will persevere in faith and good works until death. Yet this verse says that the ones on the rocky soil "believe for a while and in time of temptation fall away."

The people represented by the second soil believe the saving message of verse 12, the message Satan took great pains to snatch away from those by the wayside, "lest they should believe and be saved."

These folks believed. And thus we know they were saved, since verse 12 says that all who believe are saved.

Notice that the Lord did not say that these people *profess* to believe. He said that they believe. That is a vital distinction. Calvinists like to speak of false professors. Yet there is no profession by anyone in this parable. The Lord Jesus Christ is the one who says that the people represented by the second soil believed the saving message.

The Lord also said that these believers fell away. That is, they did not persevere, but they did believe *for a time.*

There is no time requirement on how long one must believe before salvation occurs. The moment one believes, he is saved forever. Verse 12 makes that clear, as do a host of other verses (John 3:16; 5:24; 6:35, 37, 39, 47; 11:25-27; Acts 16:30-31; Gal 2:16; Eph 2:8-9; Rev 22:17).

Did you know that of the four soils, the second soil is the only one that is specifically said to believe? We are told soil one does not believe. We are not told specifically that soils three and four believe.

Each soil is better than the one before. Soil three, for example, does not fall away. It perseveres, unlike soil two. That soil three believes is clear in that it, like soils two and four, "sprang up" (Luke 8:6-8). Springing up shows that the seed has germinated and life has begun. In addition, since soil three is better than soil two, it must not only believe, but continue in belief and not fall away.

Soil three does not bear mature fruit. Its fruitfulness is choked out by "cares, riches, and the pleasures of life" (Luke 8:14).

The final soil believes, perseveres in belief and good works, and produces an abundance of mature fruit.

Anyone Who Believes the Saving Word
Is Saved (Luke 8:11-13)

Because of this very passage Calvinism proposed something it calls "temporary faith." Faith that is temporary is any faith that fails to last a lifetime. So temporary faith can believe the saving message for a day, a year, a decade, or decades, but apostasy eventually occurs. According to Calvinism, when apostasy occurs, the person proves he never *really* believed.

David Allen and Steve Lemke and a group of Southern Baptist theologians wrote a book critiquing five-point Calvinism. The book is called *Whosoever Will*. In Chapter 6, Ken Keathley discusses temporary faith. This lengthy quote is powerful:[1]

> The doctrine of temporary faith, a notion first formulated by Calvin but later developed by Beza and William Perkins, further intensified the problem of assurance in Calvinist and Puritan theology. According to them, God gives to the reprobate, whom He never intended to save in the first place, a "taste" of His grace. Based on passages such as Matt 7:21-23; Heb

---

[1] David L. Allen and Steve W. Lemke, Editors, *Whosoever Will: A Biblical-Theological Critique of Five-Point Calvinism* (Nashville, TN: B & H Academic, 2010), 169-70.

6:4-6; and the Parable of the Sower, Beza and
Perkins attribute this false, temporary faith to
an ineffectual work of the Holy Spirit…Those
who profess to be believers are encouraged to
examine themselves lest they are found to pos-
sess only this temporary faith. Beza declared
that the reason God gives temporary faith to
the reprobate is so that "their fall might be more
grievous."[2] In Olmsted's opinion, Beza's teaching
"comes perilously close to ascribing the matter
to divine sadism."[3]

But Luke 8:11-15 directly contradicts the notion that
faith which later falters is not saving faith. In this passage
anyone who believes is saved, regardless of how long he
believes or how quickly he falls away. Only by reading
Calvinist teaching on perseverance into this passage can
one make it support Calvinism.

Remember that it is the Lord who said that the person represented by the second soil believed. It is not that
the second soil person *professed to believe*. There is no
profession mentioned. The Lord Jesus Christ indicated
that the second soil person believed the saving message.

Calvinism has a particularly hard time explaining
how the Word of God concerning salvation can be believed and a sprout can spring up and yet everlasting life
has not yet begun. Calvinists have to hem and haw and
say that *spiritual life* began, but not *everlasting life*. But

---

[2] Keathley's footnote for this citation reads, "Cited in Kendall, *Calvin and English Calvinism*, 36.
[3] See Olmstead, "Staking All on Faith's Object," 140-41 (cited by Keathley, *Whosoever Will*, 170 n.21).

spiritual life is everlasting life. There is no spiritual life apart from everlasting life.

Besides, the Calvinist view of total depravity means the unregenerate can do absolutely nothing of spiritual value. If so, what is this faith and what is this springing up?

The springing up shows that everlasting life is now possessed.

In addition, the Calvinist view of our temporary faith contradicts its view of total depravity. Remember the cadavers at the bottom of the well who couldn't grab the rope? Now Calvinists have to say that the cadaver can grab the rope, but only for a time (days, months, years, decades). But how can a cadaver grab a rope? Calvinists can't have it both ways.

Even Apostasy Can't Undo the New Birth

The point of soil two is that even apostasy cannot undo the new birth. To say that soil two argues *against* the possibility of apostasy is like saying the Titanic proves that ships can't sink.

The Lord was warning that apostasy is possible. There is no other way to understand the second soil and still accept what the Lord said about it.

And since everlasting life cannot be lost, the Lord was saying that apostasy cannot undo the new birth.

Conclusion

Luke 8:12 contradicts Calvinism. The seed germinated in a soil that failed to persevere to the end in faith and good works. The second soil believed for a time, then later fell away; but it had already germinated. The plant had already sprung up. Life had already begun. And since everlasting life is ever-lasting life, the life continued even in the face of apostasy.

The third soil doesn't directly contradict Calvinism, but it puts a strain on its application of the perseverance of the saints. The third soil perseveres in faith, and even perseveres in good works, to a limited degree. But the third soil does not produce *mature fruit*. It lacks the abundance of fruit that Calvinism has come to say is true of all believers.

Calvinists should take heart, however, in the fact that the Parable of the Four Soils does support the preservation of the saints. The moment a person believes in Jesus for everlasting life, he is saved once and for all whether he perseveres or not. That is what the Lord and His Apostles taught. That is the promise of life (1 Tim 4:8; 2 Tim 1:1; Titus 1:2; 1 John 1:1).

Luke 8:11-15 shows that Calvinism, though well-intentioned, is incompatible with the Bible.

CHAPTER 10

Preservation Guaranteed After One Drink (John 4:13-15)

THE FIFTH POINT OF CALVINISM teaches (in part) that God *preserves* only those who *persevere* in faith and good works until death. Consequently, according to Calvinism, a person cannot be certain he will be preserved because he cannot be sure that he will persevere.

If there is a single passage in the Bible which indicates that at the moment one believes in Christ he is secure forever, or that guarantees preservation of the saints independent of their perseverance, then Calvinism collapses. And that is precisely what Jesus taught the woman at the well in John 4:13-15.

Just One Drink (John 4:13-14)

According to Calvinism, John 4:13-15 should link preservation (eternal security) with perseverance. Yet the Lord did not say anything about perseverance. He said, "whoever drinks of the water I shall give him will never thirst."

When the Lord said, "Whoever drinks of this water will thirst again," He was speaking of everyone. The need to drink is universal. We can't just load up on water today and never need to drink again.

Similarly, when the Lord Jesus said, "whoever drinks of that water I shall give him will never thirst," He was speaking of everyone and anyone. Anyone who drinks this living water will never thirst again. Unlike a drink of regular water, one drink of the special water and the need to keep on drinking ceases forever. One drink forever quenches the thirst.

And the woman's response, found in verse 15, makes it clear that she understood that perseverance was not required.

One Drink and You Will Never
Need to Draw Water Again (John 4:15)

Lest there be any doubt that is what He meant, the woman repeated what she understood Him to mean: "Sir, give me this water, that I may not thirst, nor come here to draw." She was thinking in physical terms, not spiritual terms. (So, by the way, was Nicodemus in John 3:4, when he asked the Lord, "How can a man be born when he is old? Can he enter a second time into his mother's womb and be born?"). The woman clearly understood the promise that if she drinks this living water, then she will never need to drink or draw water again.

Notice, too, that the Lord did not correct her understanding regarding the permanence of the gift received. But He did go on to correct her mistaken idea that He was speaking of physical water and physical thirst.

The Lord came back to this motif when He was giving His Bread of Life sermon in John 6. There He said, "I am the bread of life. He who comes to Me shall never hunger, and *he who believes in Me shall never thirst*" (John 6:35, emphasis added). He did not say that the person who *keeps on believing* in Him shall never thirst. He said that the person who *believes* in Him *now* shall never thirst later. This is an obvious statement of eternal security of the one who believes now, not of the one who will keep on believing and believing and believing.

If the Lord was promising what Calvinism says, then He would have said, *Woman, if you keep on believing in Me until you die, then you shall never thirst after that again. Your whole life you will have to be careful to keep on believing in Me. Just as you come here daily to draw physical water, you need to keep on drinking the water of life each day in order to retain everlasting life. But once you die, the need to drink will be over. Persevere in belief and you will then become secure forever.*

Then the woman at the well would have said something like, "Sir, give me this water and show me how I can get it each day until I die so that I might not thirst in eternity."

Of course, even that wouldn't reflect the Calvinist position, would it? According to Calvinism one must persevere in both faith *and good works* in order to obtain everlasting life. But the Lord didn't speak of the need of perseverance in either faith or good works.

"He Who Believes in Me" Doesn't Mean "He Who Keeps on Believing in Me"

The Lord told the woman at the well that she had to drink this living water to get everlasting life. Later He said, "Woman, believe Me…" When she left her waterpot (the old water, as opposed to the living water) behind, she went to the men of the village and evangelized the villagers. She led many to faith in Christ.

The living water is the message that Jesus is the Christ Who guarantees everlasting life to all who believe in Him. Compare John 4:16-26. By revealing details about her past that no stranger could know, the Lord convinced her that He indeed is the Messiah (vv 25-26). Then it all came together for her: This Man is the Messiah and all who believe in Him have everlasting life.

The Lord here compared drinking with believing. To drink the living water He offers as a free gift (John 4:10) is to believe in Him (John 6:35, "he who believes in Me shall never thirst").

Let's say that the woman or Jesus or both of them drank some of the water she had drawn. That would have occurred *at a point in time*. Would they thirst again? Of course. That is what Jesus meant when He said, "Whoever drinks of this water will thirst again."

So, too, the figurative drinking of living water occurs *at a point in time*. The moment one drinks *that water*, he will never thirst again: "whoever drinks of the water that I shall give him will never thirst."

Notice that the living water is not everlasting life. Instead, it is the message of life. Once we believe the message of life, we have everlasting life: "the water that I shall give him will become in him a fountain of water springing up into everlasting life." Drinking the water results in everlasting life. That is, believing in Jesus results in everlasting life.

Not a lifetime of drinking. Not a lifetime of believing. While we obviously should continue to believe the promise of life and should live God-honoring lives, our eternal destiny does not depend on what we do after we believe in Jesus. The moment we believe in Him, we become eternally secure. Our eternal destiny relies solely on *His faithfulness to His promise.*

The Apostle Paul said the same thing in Eph 2:8-9:

> For by grace you have been saved through faith, and that not of yourselves; it is the gift of God, not of works, lest anyone should boast.

The words "you have been saved" refer to a past completed action that has an abiding result (perfect tense, passive voice). The believers in Ephesus *had already been saved* by God once and for all. Their salvation did not depend on their persevering in their faith or persevering in good works. Indeed, Paul said that their salvation was by God's grace (His favor) through faith, apart from works.[1]

---

[1] Some point to Eph 2:10 to try to say that all who are truly born-again will persevere in good works. But they fail to notice the change in pronouns. In Eph 2:8-9 the pronouns are second person plural. Paul uses *you* and *yourselves* in those verses. Then in verse 10 he shifts to the first person plural, *we*: "For we are His workman, created in Christ Jesus for good works, which God prepared beforehand that we should walk in them." Why the shift from *you* to *we*? In Ephesians *we* refers to the Church, Jews and Gentiles together in one body. Note that Eph 2:11-22 makes this clear. The second person plural pronoun refers to the Gentile readers. Paul explicitly says this in verse 11, "Therefore remember that you, once Gentiles in the flesh…" The Church, Jews and Gentiles united

The salvation of the believers in Ephesus was completed and secure the moment they came to faith in Christ for everlasting life.

Whoever Means All Can Believe and Have Everlasting Life (John 4:13-14)

Jerry Vines says that the word *whoever* is used in John's Gospel

> to emphasize that there are no limits on who may believe...it is the design of the sovereign God to make the salvation of all people possible and to secure the salvation of all who believe. What kind of God would not make salvation possible for all?[2]

Whoever drinks well water will thirst again. Whoever drinks Jesus' living water, the promise of life, will never thirst again. The illustration the Lord uses in John 4 contradicts Calvinism. Just as everyone is free to drink regular water, so all are free to drink living water.

Conclusion

Who is born again? Is it the person who believes in Jesus in a moment, or is it the person who keeps on

---

in one body, has been created by God to produce good works. Of course that should be true of every local church. However, this is in no way a guarantee that every local church will accomplish what God wishes for it. Still less is Paul promising that all individual believers will persevere in good works.

[2] David L. Allen and Steve W. Lemke, *Whosoever Will* (Nashville, TN: B&H Academic, 2010), 24.

believing in Jesus forever? If the answer is that perseverance in faith is required, then the Lord Jesus misled the woman at the well. Indeed, if that were true then He misled people over and over again by saying that anyone who *right now* believes in Him has everlasting life that can never be lost.

Did you notice as you read John 4 that John doesn't tell us if she stopped living in sin? Wouldn't that be inexplicable if the Lord and the Apostle John had believed Calvinism's perseverance of the saints?

Did she continue in faith? We are not told here or anywhere in John or the rest of the NT. Did the Samaritan men who came to faith persevere? We are not told. Those are not arguments *from silence* but *about silence.*

Is Calvinism Biblical? John 4:13-15 is yet another indication that it is not.

Perseverance of the Saints

CHAPTER 11

The Basis of Condemnation Is Unbelief, Not Lack of Perseverance (Revelation 20:11-15)

ACCORDING TO THE FIFTH POINT of Calvinism, only those who persevere in faith and good works will gain entrance into Christ's kingdom. Thus if a believer falls away prior to death, he will be eternally condemned.

One would think that, under this scheme, as long as faith continued until death, that person would go to be with the Lord regardless of his works. However, Calvinism links perseverance to both faith *and works*. Thus if either fails, the person ends up eternally condemned.

Moreover, it is not really possible in Calvinism to know if you believe in Jesus or not. For the Calvinist, saving faith is more than being convinced that Jesus guarantees the eternal destiny of believers, because even the non-elect can believe that.

In their minds, saving faith is some mystical thing which includes being persuaded of certain truths, but which also obeys God and perseveres in that obedience until death.

In the foreword to a recent book by Tom Schreiner on justification by faith alone, John Piper made this fascinating comment which is, as far as I can tell, unique among Calvinists:

> As Tom Schreiner says, the book "tackles one of the fundamental questions of our human condition: how can a person be right with God?"
>
> The stunning Christian answer is: *sola fide*—[by] faith alone. But be sure you hear this carefully and precisely: He says *right with God* by faith alone, not *attain heaven* by faith alone. There are other conditions for attaining heaven, but no others for entering a right relationship to God. In fact, one must already be in right relationship with God by faith alone in order to meet the other conditions.[1]

What are these *other conditions*, plural? Piper goes on to say that they are "love and obedience—inherent righteousness."[2]

Under this way of looking at it, you can't be sure you are right with God *now*, because you can't be sure you have real faith. And in addition, you can't be sure you will gain entrance into Christ's kingdom *then*, because you can't be

---

[1] Thomas Schreiner, *Faith Alone—The Doctrine of Justification* (Grand Rapids, MI: Zondervan, 2015), 11, emphasis Piper's.
[2] Ibid.

sure that when you die you will have met the other conditions of love, obedience, and personal righteousness either.

It is clear in Piper's comment and Schreiner's book that many Calvinists believe that the basis of escaping eternal condemnation will be our works. Calvinists believe that the Judgment Seat of Christ (2 Cor 5:9-10) is another name for the Great White Throne Judgment (Rev 20:11-15). In their view, there will be a single final judgment of all people—of believers and unbelievers—and only at that judgment will people learn their final destiny, the kingdom or the lake of fire.

According to the Calvinist understanding of Rev 20:11-15, what is found in the books of deeds determines who gets into the kingdom and who is sent to the lake of fire.

Thus, most Calvinists inspect their works and hope to find enough good ones to convince them they will persevere in faithfulness until death. But since their works are imperfect, and since they have years or decades left during which they might fall, they must deal with ongoing doubt. That is why David Engelsma calls Puritanism, the English branch of Calvinism, "a gospel of doubt."[3] He says,

> Puritan [English Calvinist] preaching…is forever questioning your assurance, forever challenging your right to assurance, forever sending you on a quest for assurance, and forever instilling doubt.[4]

---

[3] David J. Engelsma, *The Gift of Assurance* (South Holland, IL: The Evangelism Committee of the Protestant Reformed Church, 2009), 53.
[4] Ibid.

The many promises of everlasting life to the one who believes in Jesus show that doubt has no place in the life of someone who believes what God says (e.g., John 3:16; 5:24; 6:35; 11:25-27; 20:30-31; Acts 16:30-31; Eph 2:8-9; 1 Tim 1:16; Rev 22:17). Doubt is unbelief. Calvinism produces doubts because it points people not to the Lord Jesus Christ and what He has promised, but to oneself.

For the Calvinist, the question is not "Will Jesus be faithful to His promise?" Instead the question is, "Will I be faithful to my promise?"[5]

Revelation 20:11-15 deals with the final judgment *of unbelievers* at the Great White Throne Judgment. It confirms the promise of life and shows that our assurance is to be found in believing what Jesus said, not in our works.

The Great White Throne Judgment: Books and a Book (Rev 20:11-12)

> Then I saw a great white throne and Him who sat on it, from whose face the earth and the heaven fled away. And there was found no place for them. And I saw the dead, small and great, standing before God, and books were opened. And another book was opened, which is the Book of Life. And the dead were judged according to their works, by the things which were written in the books (Rev 20:11–12).

---

[5] For many Calvinists, saving faith includes a promise to obey God. For example, see Wayne Grudem, *Free Grace Theology: 5 Ways It Diminishes the Gospel* (Wheaton, IL: Crossway, 2016), 99-118. See esp. 106, 110.

Since all Christians will be judged *before* the Millennium begins (2 Cor 5:1-11), this judgment refers to the evaluation of all the *unbelievers* of all time (plus possibly believers from the Millennium).

Notice there are books (plural) that contain all "their works," and a Book (singular), the Book of Life, which contains a list of all who have everlasting life. The *books* must not be confused with *the Book.*

All at this judgment will be "judged according to their works." That is a common theme in the New Testament (Matt 16:27; 2 Tim 4:14; 1 Pet 1:17; Rev 2:23; 18:6). God will fairly recompense all, believers and unbelievers alike.

The text does not indicate what the outcome of looking at the books will be, but it does specify the outcome of looking at the Book (Rev 20:15).

Based on other Scripture, the reason why the works of unbelievers are judged is twofold: 1) to show that no one has a claim to enter the kingdom based on sinlessness (Rom 3:23; 6:23) and 2) to reveal how much torment each unbeliever has earned for the works he did in this life (Matt 10:11-15; 11:21-24).

Is Rev 20:15 consistent with Calvinism? Let's see.

The Book of Life Determines
Eternal Destiny (Rev 20:15)

And anyone not found written in the Book of Life was cast into the lake of fire.

According to Calvinism the basis of escaping eternal condemnation is perseverance in faith *and good works.*

Unbelievers lack sufficient works to prove they had true faith and therefore suffer eternal condemnation.

Thus, if Calvinism were true, Rev 20:15 would read, "And anyone whose works failed to prove that he had genuinely believed in Jesus was cast into the lake of fire." The issue would be what was found in the books, not what was found or not found in the Book of Life.

Instead, according to Rev 20:15, the basis of eternal condemnation is *not being found in the Book of Life*. Works have nothing to do with that. The Book of Life contains a list of all who have everlasting life. All who lack everlasting life are cast into the lake of fire. All with everlasting life get into Christ's eternal kingdom.

We know from the Lord Jesus' teaching what one must do to get into the Book of Life. He taught that whoever believes in Him has everlasting life and will never experience the second death of Rev 20:14 (e.g., John 3:16; 5:24; 6:35; 11:26, "shall never die" = "shall never experience the second death").

Dave Hunt accurately comments, "Anyone who will spend eternity in the Lake of Fire (Revelation 20:14) has sent himself there by rejecting the salvation God has provided for him as a free gift of His grace."[6]

If you are in the Book, then you are secure, right now and forever, *no matter what.* You do not need to wait to see if you persevere to find out if you have everlasting life. Your assurance is not based on your works or your feelings. It is based on your faith in Christ. Period.

Revelation 20:11-15 contradicts Calvinism.

---

[6] Dave Hunt, *What Love Is This? Calvinism's Misrepresentation of God,* Second Edition (Bend, OR: The Berean Call, 2004), 312.

CHAPTER 12

Assurance Is Independent of Perseverance (John 11:25-27)

THE FIFTH POINT OF CALVINISM, the P in TULIP, concerns both the preservation of the saints (eternal security) and the perseverance of the saints. According to Calvinism, only those who are persevering in faith and good works at the time of their death will be preserved.

Thus, according to Calvinism, assurance is found in your perseverance over your lifetime. If you fall away at some point and fail to repent before you die, you show that you were not eternally secure. More on that in a moment.

Do we find that teaching in John 11:25-27? Jesus' interaction with Martha is an excellent test case for the fifth point of Calvinism.

Assurance of Resurrection Is by Faith Alone, Not by Perseverance in Faith or Works (John 11:25)

> Jesus said to her, "I am the resurrection and the life. He who believes in Me, though he may die, he shall live" (John 11:25).

The Lord was making two related, but not identical, promises in verses 25-26. Promise one is found in the last half of verse 25. Promise two is found in verse 26.

The two promises are directly tied to the "I am" statement the Lord made at the start of verse 25: "I am (1) the resurrection and (2) the life."

The expression "I am the resurrection" means that Jesus is in some way associated with the resurrection of the dead. This might refer to His own resurrection. However, the second half of verse 25 shows He was actually speaking of the resurrection of believers: "He who believes in Me, though he may die [physically], he shall live [physically]." The Lord was not talking about spiritual death and spiritual life here, but about physical death and future bodily resurrection.

All believers will have glorified bodies (cf. 2 Cor 5:1-8). The basis of assurance is solely faith in Christ. Works are not at all the issue. The moment a person believes in Christ, he is guaranteed he will have a glorified body forever. Perseverance in faith and good works is not required for eternal security. Anyone who believes in Jesus is sure to be in the kingdom in a glorified body.

That doesn't fit with Calvinist teaching. Neither does verse 26.

Assurance You'll Never Die Spiritually Is by Faith Alone (John 11:26)

"'And whoever lives and believes in Me shall never die. Do you believe this?'" (John 11:26).

Remember the second part of Jesus' "I am" statement in verse 25? He said, "I am…the life." Clearly this statement in verse 26 is related to *everlasting life*. Jesus is everlasting life (cf. 1 John 1:2; 5:20). In addition, He gives everlasting life to all who simply believe in Him: "And whoever lives and believes in Me shall never die." The words *shall never die* are another way of saying that the believer will never experience the second death, being cast into the lake of fire (Rev 20:14-15). Once a person has everlasting life, he has it forever. It cannot be lost.

Calvinism *formally* agrees. It says that whoever has everlasting life cannot lose it. But Calvinism also says that if a believer falls away and does not return before death, then he will be eternally condemned. How can that be?

Calvinism suggests that there are two types of people who believe in Jesus. Both are persuaded about key truths about Jesus, but only one of the two will persevere in good works, and that person is the *true believer*. The believer who fails to persevere is the *false believer*. But Calvinism calls both of them *believers*.

While Calvinism formally affirms eternal security, practically speaking, it provides no comfort or assurance, because no one knows if he might die in sin and end up eternally condemned.

One Calvinist pastor and seminary professor explained it to me in this way:

I see in my life what I believe are the works of
the Holy Spirit. However, I realize I might fail to
persevere. If so, then I will prove what I thought
were the works of the Spirit were not, and I will
end up in hell forever.

That pastor and professor pointed to 1 Cor 9:27. He
said it clearly shows Paul was not certain that he would
persevere. He said, *if the Apostle Paul was not sure that
he would persevere, then surely we cannot be sure that we
will persevere either.*

He has a good point...*if* Paul was speaking about assurance of having eternal life. But Paul's actual concern
was with his eternal rewards, not his eternal destiny.
Since eternal rewards do depend on perseverance, Paul
was right to be uncertain of the outcome.

But in Martha's case, the subject was everlasting life.
And the basis of assurance the Lord gave Martha was
simply faith in Him, not perseverance in faith and good
works. The clarity of Martha's response to Jesus' question, "Do you believe this?" shows that she was certain
of her eternal destiny, independent of her future actions,
unlike Calvinists today.

Martha Was Sure Apart from Perseverance, Yet the Lord Did Not Rebuke Her (John 11:27)

She said to Him, "Yes, Lord, I believe that You
are the Christ, the Son of God, who is to come
into the world"(John 11:27).

Martha's answer is inconsistent with Calvinism. Calvinists do not know if they believe in Jesus or not. They

hope they do. They look for evidence in their works that they believe in Jesus. But they do not know if they are secure or not.

One day when I was in Southern California visiting my Mom, I heard two Calvinists on a radio program talking about assurance. They discussed how we might have assurance that we are elect, i.e., assurance that we will spend eternity with the Lord.

The talk show hosts indicated that assurance is a difficult thing to obtain because it involves analyzing our actions and our feelings. Do our actions and feelings, fallible though they are, give sufficient indication that we are probably among the elect?

At this point a man called in. He said something like this: *You guys don't make sense. I know I'll spend eternity with the Lord because I believe in Jesus and He said that whoever believes in Him has everlasting life and will never perish. It is quite simple. It is not difficult like you are saying.*

To this the hosts replied, *Yes, but how do you know you really believe? That is the point we are making. Sure, you believe some correct Bible doctrines. But saving faith is more than intellectual assent. It involves surrender and obedience. Those things are seen in your works and your works are not perfect. Hence assurance is difficult to obtain. And only those who persevere until death prove they truly believe. So, ultimately, while we can and should be confident that we are probably saved, we cannot be sure.*

Martha was like the caller, not the radio hosts. She knew she believed in Jesus and told Him so.

"Yes, Lord," would have been a sufficient answer. But Martha went on to explain *why* she knew that Jesus would raise all believers and *why* she knew that He gives all believers everlasting life that can never be lost. He does that because He is *the Christ, the Son of God, the one who was prophesied to come into the world.*

Martha said nothing about her works or about her prospects of persevering. She simply asserted that she believes what He said. And Jesus did not correct her. Nor did the Apostle John.

Clearly John used Martha's confession as a pivotal statement in his Gospel. We know this because the purpose statement in John, found in John 20:30-31, says exactly what Martha said. She said "You are the Christ, the Son of God…" John 20:31 says, "These are written that you may believe that Jesus is the Christ, the Son of God, and that [by] believing you may have life in His name." Martha affirmed the saving proposition. She believed that He is the resurrection and the life, the one who guarantees bodily resurrection and everlasting life that can never be lost to all who simply believe in Him.

All who are persuaded that Jesus is the resurrection and the life—that is, the Christ, the Son of God—have everlasting life and will never die spiritually. Perseverance is not required. All that is required is believing what Jesus promised, as Martha did.

The Present Tense for Believing Does Not Suggest That Lifelong Faith Is Required to Be Born Again

Calvinists suggest that since John 11:25-26, as well as most of the salvific verses in John, uses the present tense of the verb *believe, pisteuō*, that ongoing, persevering faith is required.

In the first place, that would mean that a person is not born again when he believes in Christ, or even before he believes, as Calvinists say. If "whoever believes in Him" means, "whoever keeps on believing in Him for his whole life," then the condition would not be met until the life ended. You couldn't say, "I was born again on September 12, 1972." You'd need to say, "I will be born again at the moment of death if I persevere in faith and good works until that time."

In the second place, that does not fit the illustrations the Lord used. One drink of the living water, or one eating of the bread of life, and you are eternally secure forever (John 4:13-15; 6:35).

In the third place, the argument is grammatically false. The present tense in the indicative mood in Greek does not refer to continuous action. The context describes what sort of action is in view with the present tense.

In addition, many of the crucial verses cited concern *articular participles*, not verbs in the indicative. An articular participle is a verbal noun.

John 11:26 shows definitely that the faith in view is a snapshot at a moment in time, not a movie of a lifetime. We know this because there *the believing one* is joined by *and* (*kai* in Greek) with *the living one*. If we know that *the living one* captures a moment in time, then so does *the believing one*.

The Lord told Martha, "Whoever lives and believes in Me shall never die" (John 11:26). The Lord was talking about eternal security there. The one who lives and believes in Him *will never die spiritually*, that is, will never experience the second death, being cast into the lake of fire (Rev 20:14).

The expression "Whoever lives and believes in Me" in John 11:26 is a parallel construction in Greek. That is, there are two present participles there with only one article. Literally the Greek says, "Every living and believing [person] in Me will never die." *Living and believing* have but one article: *pas ho zōn kai pisteuōn eis eme.*

Therefore, if the Calvinist says that believing must be continuous since the present tense of the participle is used, then so must the living be continuous since the present tense of the participle is used. Thus Calvinism says that John 11:26 means, "*Whoever keeps on living forever and keeps on believing in Me forever shall never die.*" Thus there would never be a point at which a person would be eternally secure, because if he ever stopped believing—or if he ever stopped living physically—then he would also die spiritually.

Plainly the Lord was saying that any living human being (*ho zōn*) who believes (*ho...pisteuōn*) in Him is eternally secure *at that very moment.* He wasn't saying that a person will become eternally secure if he never dies and if he never stops believing. He wasn't even discussing when that person first believed and gained everlasting life. He was saying that if you find a living human who believes in Jesus, you've found someone who has everlasting life.

Any living human being who believes in Jesus will never die spiritually. The Lord Jesus guarantees it.

Contra Calvinism, Certainty Is Correct

Jesus' interaction with Martha contradicts Calvinism. There is no certainty of everlasting life in Calvinism prior to death. The Calvinist *hopes* he will persevere in faith and good works, but can't be *sure* he will.

But Martha was sure of her eternal destiny and the Lord did not correct her. The Lord Jesus wanted her to be sure. He wants all who believe in Him to be sure of their eternal destiny.

The Calvinist is not sure that he is elect, that Christ died for Him, that God has irresistibly drawn him, that he will persevere, or that he is eternally secure. Calvinist theologian David Engelsma sadly calls the Calvinism of most adherents today "a gospel of doubt."[1]

[1] David J. Engelsma, *The Gift of Assurance* (South Holland, IL: Evangelism Committee of the Protestant Reformed Church, 2009), 53.

Conclusion

CALVINISM IS A LOGICAL SYSTEM OF THOUGHT that was devised not by John Calvin, but by those who followed him. While logical, the five, or six, points of Calvinism are not Biblical.

Scripture crushes Calvinism. In this book we looked at twelve key verses that show that Calvinism is not consistent with the Word of God.

The Calvinist understanding of total depravity is disproved by John 6:35 and by the account of Cornelius coming to faith in Christ in Acts 10.

The second point, unconditional election, is inconsistent with passages like Acts 13:46 and John 5:39-40, which show that people who are closed to Jesus and His promise of life do not come to faith, and those who are open do.

Limited atonement, or particular redemption, is ruled out by John 1:29 and 2 Pet 2:1. Jesus removed the sin barrier for all of mankind. Christ bought everyone, including unbelieving false teachers bound for the lake of fire.

The fourth point, irresistible grace, is inconsistent with passages like John 12:32 and Matt 23:37-39. The cross of Christ is a message that the Lord uses to draw all to Him. Jesus wanted to set up His kingdom in the first century, but the Jews of Jerusalem and Israel were unwilling. He was drawing and they were resisting.

The fifth point (or the fifth and six points) is the preservation of the saints and the perseverance of the saints. We looked at four passages which show that perseverance is not guaranteed and that preservation is not dependent on perseverance: Luke 8:11-13; John 4:13-15; Rev 20:11-15; and John 11:25-27.

An issue which emerged often in our brief study of Calvinism is that if you buy into the Calvinist way of thinking, then you do not have assurance that you will spend eternity with the Lord. You will forever wonder, "Did Jesus die for me?" "Am I one of the elect?" and "Will I persevere to the end of my life and make it into the kingdom?".

If you are not a Calvinist, I hope you have been persuaded all who simply believe in Christ have everlasting life which can never be lost.

If you are a Calvinist, I hope you have been persuaded of the same truth, that all who simply believe in Christ have everlasting life which can never be lost.

There is no other way to be born again. The only way is through faith in Christ, apart from works.

Knowing that you are eternally secure is an extremely powerful motivation to live for God. He has given us so much. And it was at the cost of His very life. We did nothing to earn it or to keep it. We simply received the free gift by believing in Him for the life He promises.

My hope for you and for me is that we fall more and more in love with the Lord Jesus Christ. I believe the truths presented in this book, that is, truths found clearly in the Bible, can help us do just that (2 Cor 3:18).

Appendices

Calvinist Responses to These Twelve Key Verses

THERE ARE MANY ACADEMIC BOOKS that carefully lay out all the Calvinist arguments for and against these twelve verses.

I wrote this book with the idea that these twelve verses test Calvinism. I dealt with the texts, not with the philosophical arguments for or against Calvinism.

In this chapter I could easily give ten or more pages of Calvinist arguments and Free Grace responses on each of the twelve texts. However, I feel it will be more powerful to limit the discussion. I fear people getting bored over lengthy quotes and counter arguments. Less is often more.

My point in this chapter is to show the Calvinist explanations of these texts are either inadequate or, in many cases, actually contradict Calvinism itself. Let's see that in action.

Faith Precedes Regeneration (John 6:35)

Calvinists often do not comment on the fact that it is those who eat the bread of life and drink the water of life who have everlasting life. In other words, the eating and the drinking (i.e., the faith) precedes receiving everlasting life. But if, as Calvinists claim, regeneration actually precedes faith, then what does the Lord mean in John 6:35?

To his credit, John Piper has commented on what the text actually says without seeming to filter his remarks through his Calvinist grid:

> In John 6:35…Jesus said, "I am the bread of life; whoever comes to me shall not hunger, and whoever believes in me shall never thirst." Coming to Jesus as the bread of life to still the hunger of your soul is the same as believing in him. That's what believing is. It is being satisfied with all that God is for us in Jesus…
>
> So the pervasive offer of this chapter from beginning to end is: Anyone may have eternal life if they will receive Jesus and trust in Jesus and treasure Jesus and be satisfied with all that God is for them in Jesus. *Whoever* feeds on my flesh—that is, whoever *believes* in me—has eternal life. I abide in you and my life becomes your life—forever.[1]

The Calvinist *answer* to John 6:35 (if there is one), seems to be to point to John 6:37 and John 6:44, which

---

[1] John Piper, "It Is the Spirit That Gives Life," December 13, 2009. See http://www.desiringgod.org/messages/it-is-the-spirit-that-gives-life. Accessed July 21, 2017. Emphasis his.

refer to the fact that the only ones who come to faith in Jesus are those whom the Father draws to Him. Yet after citing John 6:37 and 6:44 and arguing that God only draws the elect, D. A. Carson then adds this enigmatic statement,

> Yet despite the strong predestinarian strain, it must be insisted with no less vigour that John emphasizes the responsibility of people to come to Jesus and can excoriate them for refusing to do so (e.g. 5:40).[2]

Calvinists do not seem to have an explanation for John 6:35, other than one which inadvertently contradicts Calvinism.

The Unregenerate Can Respond to God (Acts 10:4)

The account of Cornelius coming to faith and being born again is a major problem for Calvinist doctrine. How do Calvinist scholars respond?

John MacArthur thinks that there is a mystery involved:

> God responds to the willing, open heart. Election never violates volition; they always go together. I don't know how they do, but God knows. Cornelius was sovereignly chosen by God, but he also had a searching heart. God reached down and gave him

---

[2] D. A. Carson, *The Gospel According to John* (Grand Rapids, MI: Eerdmans, 1991), 293.

the disposition to turn and seek Him even when he
was dead in his trespasses and sins (Eph. 2:1).[3]

According to the Calvinist understanding of total
depravity, those who are dead in trespasses and sins
cannot seek God. Yet when faced with a Biblical example
of an unregenerate man who seeks God, the Calvinist
admits that it is true, but fails to change his theology.

People Judge Themselves Worthy or Unworthy of Everlasting Life (Acts 13:46)

Paul's words in Acts 13:46 are inconsistent with Calvinism. How, then, do Calvinists explain what Paul said?

Calvinist Alexander Maclaren (1826-1910) wrote
concerning Acts 13:46:

Note the reason for turning to the Gentiles.
The Jews by their rejection of the word "judged
themselves unworthy of eternal life"…The
phrase says nothing about their estimation of
themselves. Probably no man in that crowd
deemed himself unworthy of life eternal; but all
unconsciously had declared themselves unfitted
for it by turning away from Christ…It is ever
solemnly true that the unbeliever passes sen-
tence on himself.[4]

---

[3] See https://www.gty.org/library/sermons-library/1734/the-salvation-of-
the-gentiles-part-1. Accessed July 21, 2017.

[4] Alexander Maclaren, *The Acts of the Apostles*, (London: Hodder and
Stoughton, 1894), 179.

While that is a good explanation of the text, it is at the same time inconsistent with at least two of the points of Calvinism, total depravity and unconditional election.

I appreciate an honest explanation of the text. But it actually underscores that Acts 13:46 is inconsistent with Calvinism.

People Unwilling to Come to Jesus for Everlasting Life (John 5:39-40)

John Piper uses this passage to tell born-again people that they should love the entire Bible, not just the New Testament.[5] But he does not discuss at all the issue of the unregenerate listeners' ability to search the Scripture or of the fact that they are not willing to come to Jesus to have everlasting life.

In his book, *Ashamed of the Gospel*, John MacArthur quotes John 5:40 to show human responsibility. He also cites a number of other passages which he suggests teach God's sovereignty. In the paragraph in which he cites John 5:40, MacArthur suggests that "our Lord combined both divine sovereignty and human responsibility."[6] Of course, this raises the problem of "how both of those two realities can be true simultaneously cannot be understood by the human mind—only by God."[7] That is inconsistent Calvinism. How can the unregenerate be responsible to believe in Jesus when according to Calvinism they cannot do that?

---

[5] See http://www.desiringgod.org/messages/if-you-believed-moses-you-would-believe-me. Accessed July 21, 2017.

[6] John MacArthur, *Ashamed of the Gospel: When the Church Becomes Like the World*, 3rd ed. (Wheaton, IL: Crossway, 2010), 166.

[7] Ibid.

Calvinist Leon Morris says concerning John 5:39-40, "'you refuse to come to me for life'…stresses the activity of the will."[8] That is following the same line as MacArthur, without explaining how that is compatible with Calvinism.

Calvinist D. A. Carson also speaks of the Jews' refusal "to come to Jesus for life," though he, too, fails to explain how this unwillingness fits within Calvinist doctrine.[9]

J. Ramsey Michaels, also a Calvinist, makes this outstanding comment on John 5:39-40: "By rejecting him [Jesus], they strangle the life-giving power of their own Scriptures."[10] However, that comment is not consistent with Calvinism.

I could not find a Calvinist who explains how John 5:39-40 fits Calvinism. At best they say that there is a mystery of how the unregenerate are responsible for their unwillingness to believe in Christ when according to Calvinism they are constitutionally unable to believe.

Christ Takes Away the Sins of the Whole World (John 1:29)

The *New Geneva Study Bible* has an explanation of John 1:29 that is far from a clear statement regarding limited atonement,

> **who takes away the sin of the world.** The "world" designated humanity in its hostility to God, as elsewhere in this Gospel. Although not

---

[8] Leon Morris, *John*, NICNT (Grand Rapids, MI: Eerdmans, 1989), 331
[9] Carson, *John*, 264.
[10] J. Ramsey Michaels, *John*, NICNT (Grand Rapids, MI: Eerdmans, 2010), 332.

all persons without exception will be saved, the sacrifice is the only atonement for human sin, and its effectiveness is not limited by time or place.[11]

John Calvin was not a Calvinist. Modern Calvinism was developed after he died. Calvin scholars debate whether he believed in the third point of Calvinism. The following comment from his commentary on John does not fit modern Calvinism:

> And when he says *the sin of the world* he extends this kindness indiscriminately to the whole human race, so that the Jews might not think the Redeemer had been sent to them alone. From this we infer that the whole world is bound in the same condemnation; and that since all men without exception are guilty of unrighteousness before God, they have need of reconciliation. John, therefore, by speaking about the sin of the world in general, wanted to make us feel our own misery and exhort us to seek the remedy. Now it is for us to embrace the blessing offered to all, that each may make up his mind that there is nothing to hinder him from finding reconciliation in Christ if only, led by faith, he comes to Him.[12]

Calvinism does not have a convincing explanation of John 1:29.

---

[11] *New Geneva Study Bible* (Nashville, TN: Thomas Nelson, 1995), 1661.
[12] John Calvin, *John* (Wheaton, IL: Crossway, 1994), 37, emphasis his.

False Teachers Who Deny the Lord
Who Bought Them (2 Peter 2:1)

According to the middle point of Calvinism, *limited atonement* (also called *particular redemption*), Christ only died for "the elect." Thus Christ died only for those who will spend eternity with Him in His kingdom.

Peter prophesied in 2 Peter 2 about coming false teachers "for whom is reserved the blackness of darkness forever" (2 Pet 2:17). The expression "the blackness of darkness forever" refers to the lake of fire.

In verse 1 Peter said something no Calvinist would ever say of people who will spend eternity in the lake of fire: "There will be false teachers among you, who will secretly bring in destructive heresies, *even denying the Lord who bought them*, and bring on themselves swift destruction" (emphasis added). Christ "bought" (*agorazō*, a term of redemption) these unregenerate false teachers who are bound for eternal condemnation.

John Piper says,

> The first thing we learn about them is that they are denying the Master who bought them. What does this mean? As with most heresies, Jesus Christ is in some way being diminished. Some aspect of his personhood or his work is being denied. But Peter never tells us what aspect. In fact, you get the impression from chapter 2 that the error of the false teachers was an error in morality, not doctrine. But the two are never really separate. How you live and how you esteem Christ always rise and fall together. It is possible to live in such a disobedient way that Christ is

scorned and belittled by our very behavior. That
seems to be what was happening here.[13]

Piper fails to explain how a person destined for the
lake of fire can have been bought by Christ. He explains
what it means to deny the Lord. He even goes on to
discuss what it means to be bought by Christ. But he
ignores the elephant in the room: 2 Peter 2:1 teaches
unlimited atonement and contradicts Calvinism.

John MacArthur gives a lengthy answer when faced
with trying to explain how Christ bought these false
teachers bound for hell. First he explains his understanding of unlimited atonement, that "His death was a poten-
tial sacrifice or atonement that becomes an actual atonement when a sinner repents and believes the gospel."[14]
Then he rejects that position because it posits that "the
Lord Jesus Christ died to make salvation possible, not
actual." Then he proceeds to defend the Calvinist idea of
total depravity (the T in TULIP) and that "salvation is
solely from God."

After all that, without having yet explained what it
means that Christ bought these unregenerate false teachers, he says,

> For whom did Christ die? He died for all who
> would believe because they were chosen, called,
> justified, and granted repentance and faith by

---

[13] John Piper, "Destruction Is Not Sleeping." See http://www.desiringgod.
org/messages/destruction-is-not-sleeping. Accessed July 21, 2017.
[14] Quoted in http://www.middletownbiblechurch.org/reformed/maca-
tone.htm. Accessed July 13, 2017. The article is entitled, "John MacArthur's Position on the Extent of the Atonement as Compared to the
IFCA Doctrinal Statement." The material quoted in notes 14 and 15 is
from MacArthur's commentary on 2 Peter and Jude (2005).

the Father. The atonement is limited to those who believe, who are the elect of God. Any believer who does not believe in universal salvation knows Christ's atonement is limited (cf. Matt. 7:13; 8:12; 10:28; 22:13; 25:46; Mark 9:43, 49; John 3:17-18; 8:24; 2 Thess. 1:7–9). Anyone who rejects the notion that the whole human race will be saved believes necessarily in a limited atonement—either limited by the sinner who is sovereign, or by God who is sovereign.[15]

After a bit more discussion, including comments by Spurgeon and David Clotfelter rejecting unlimited atonement, MacArthur comes up with this totally unexplained and unsupported conclusion, "Therefore, false teachers' sins were not paid for in the atonement of Christ."

Nowhere in the article does MacArthur explain what Peter meant when he said that Christ bought these false teachers. Peter said that Christ bought these unregenerate false teachers. MacArthur declares that Christ did not buy these false teachers.

Calvinism has no good answer for 2 Pet 2:1. It is inconsistent with limited atonement.

God Is Drawing Everyone, Not Just a Few (John 12:32)

Jesus said, "And I, if I am lifted up from the earth, will draw all peoples to Myself" (John 12:32). The word *peoples* in the NKJV, or *men* or *people* in other major

---

[15] Ibid.

translations, is not actually found in the Greek. The Lord actually said, "I…will draw all to Myself." All.

Many Calvinists say that Christ's drawing cannot refer to all people, since, in the Calvinist's view, all who are drawn inevitably come to faith in Christ. Hence, if all were drawn, universalism would be true. But since universalism is not true, neither can the idea that all men are drawn to Christ. Therefore, Calvinists insist that *all* must actually refer to *some*.

This is a very common Calvinist explanation (cf. Calvin, John Gill, Matthew Henry). *All* means *some Jews* and *some Gentiles*, or, more accurately, a small percentage of Jews and of Gentiles.

John Piper suggest that *all* refers to "all his sheep, all his children, all the elect."[16] But the words *sheep*, *children*, and *the elect* are not in the verse. Nor are the words *Jews* and *Gentiles*.

D. A. Carson similarly says, "this drawing is selective…all men without distinction (i.e., not just Jews) rather than to all men without exception."[17] However, he concludes by saying, "Yet despite the strong predestinarian strain, it must be insisted with no less vigour that John emphasized the responsibility of people to come to Christ, and can excoriate them for refusing to do so (e.g., 5:40)."[18]

But if Jesus meant that He would draw a small percentage of Jews and Gentiles to Himself, then why was

---

[16] John Piper, "For This Purpose I Have Come to This Hour." See http://www.desiringgod.org/messages/for-this-purpose-i-have-come-to-this-hour. Accessed July 20, 2017.

[17] D. A. Carson, *The Gospel According to John* (Grand Rapids, MI: Eerdmans, 1991), 293.

[18] Ibid.

He so unclear? Why didn't He simply say, "I will draw a few Jews and Gentiles to Myself"? Or maybe He could have said, "I will draw elect Jews and Gentiles to Myself." (Of course, that would have been confusing since 100% of the Jews are elect. They are God's chosen people.)

The Calvinist interpretation of John 12:32 is not consistent with the rest of John's Gospel, as D. A. Carson inadvertently admits. Their interpretation is *possible in isolation*. But when compared with many other texts discussed in this book (Matt 23:37-39; John 1:9, 29; 3:16; 4:10; 5:39-40; Acts 10:1-48; 13:46; 17:11), Calvinism's interpretation of John 12:32 *is impossible*. John 12:32, like John 3:16, is a problem passage for Calvinists.

Unbelieving Israel Resisted God's Grace (Matthew 23:37-39)

According to Calvinism God sovereignly imposes His will on people, and it is impossible for humans to resist His will. While that might make a certain amount of sense philosophically, the Scriptures themselves throw a wrench into those gears.

In Matt 23:37-39, Jesus lamented how He wanted to gather the people of Jerusalem to Himself. Then He added the sad words, "But you were not willing."

The kingdom would have come in the first century for Israel if that generation had been willing to come to Jesus, that is, to believe in Him (cf. John 5:39-40). But they were not willing.

What is the Calvinist explanation?

At the Grace to You website in an April 8, 1984, message entitled, "Jesus' Last Words to Israel, Part 2 (Matt

23:37-39)," John MacArthur says some things about this passage that most Calvinists would not:

> Let me just say to those of you who tend to be hard-line Calvinists, I find no absolute determinism in this verse. I find no fate here. I find no predetermined destiny here without thought for a response. I find here that God would, but you wouldn't. That's what I find here. And somewhere in the midst of that incredible apparent paradox of sovereignty and volition, we've got to see this passage. "I would," He says. "How often I would have gathered, but you would not." And every soul that spends eternity outside the protection of God, every soul that spends eternity in hell is there because they would not, they would not.[19]

Calvinist theologian Robert Reymond says in his *Systematic Theology* that "some Reformed theologians teach that God can and does earnestly desire, ardently long to see come to pass, and actually work to effect things which has not decreed to come to pass" (p. 692, note 25). He cites John Murray and John Gerstner in this regard. Murray based this conclusion in part on Matt 23:37-39.

Reymond's response to this way of thinking is to suggest that it ultimately leads to unlimited atonement being possible and to forcing one "to impute such

---

[19] https://www.gty.org/library/sermons-library/2365/jesus-last-words-to-israel-part-2. Accessed Sept 27, 2017.

irrationality to God."[20] Reymond, however, gives no explanation of what Matt 23:37-39 actually does mean.

In his *Systematic Theology,* John Frame, after quoting this passage, says that it refers to both inability and ability: "Our inabilities are combined with abilities, so that we are convicted as willful sinners."[21] Earlier he had said, "Sinners do resist God's purposes; indeed, that is a significant theme in Scripture (Isa. 65:12; Matt. 23:37-39…). But the point of the doctrine [irresistible grace] is that their resistance does not succeed against the Lord."[22] How that makes sense in Matt 23:37-39 is not explained. Jesus would have gathered the people of Jerusalem. He did not gather them because they were not willing. They sure seem to have succeeded in delaying what the Lord wanted to do right then.

Matthew 23:37-39 is inconsistent with Calvinism.

Preservation Even If You Fall Away (Luke 8:11-15)

In Luke's report of the Parable of the Four Soils and its interpretation, he quotes the Lord as saying that the people represented by the second soil, "believed for a time, and in time of temptation fell away" (Luke 8:13). The Lord was saying that one is saved when he believes in Him (Luke 8:12) and that salvation is secure even if the believer later falls away (Luke 8:13).

---

[20] Robert Reymond, *A New Systematic Theology of the Christian Faith* (Nashville, TN: Thomas Nelson, 1998), 693, n. 25.

[21] John Frame, *Systematic Theology; An Introduction to Christian Belief* (Phillipsburg, NJ: P&R, 2013), 818.

[22] Frame, *Systematic Theology,*145.

However, Calvinists do not see it that way. That would contradict part of the fifth point of Calvinism (perseverance of the saints, the P in TULIP).

In his sermon on "The Parable of the Sower (Luke 8:1-15)," Calvinist R. C. Sproul says that the person represented by the second soil *professes to believe* in Christ,[23] *but does not actually believe.* He says that the seed "takes root for a moment" and sprouts, but then it withers and dies.[24] He calls these types of experiences "false conversions."

Yet it is not the people of the second soil who professed to believe. The Lord said nothing about profession. The Lord Jesus Himself said that "they believe for a time." Was the Lord wrong? They didn't believe, even though the Lord of glory said they did?

And how can the seed germinate and yet life not begin?

John MacArthur gives the same explanation in *The Gospel According to Jesus.* He, too, says that the second soil represents "profession(s) of faith," but "not genuine faith."[25] He says,

> The sprouting of the seed in the shallow soil and the weedy soil simply means that the Word has been received and [has] begun to operate, not that eternal life has been conferred.[26]

---

[23] See http://www.ligonier.org/learn/sermons/parable-sower-luk8/. Begin listening at 18:06*ff.*

[24] Ibid. See minute 20:55*ff.*

[25] John MacArthur, *The Gospel According to Jesus: What Is Authentic Faith?* (Grand Rapids, MI: Zondervan, 2009), 133.

[26] Ibid., 136.

But how can "the Word [have] been received" by people whom Calvinists say are non-elect (compare John 1:12-13)? Doesn't Calvinism say that the non-elect are like stones and cadavers, totally unable to respond to God? How can the Word of God have "begun to operate" in the non-elect?

And why is it that in verse 12 germination would result in salvation, but not in verse 13?

The idea that the saving word "has been received and [has] begun to operate" and yet "eternal life has [not] been conferred" doesn't make sense.

Luke 8:11-15 contradicts Calvinism.

Preservation Guaranteed After Just One Drink (John 4:13-15)

The woman at the well understood Jesus to be saying that if she drank the living water which He promised, then she would never have to come and draw water again (John 4:15). And the Lord did not correct her understanding, other than to show her that He was not talking about physical water and physical life, but spiritual water and everlasting life. But one drink would forever settle the issue of her eternal destiny as the Lord later repeated in John 6:35.

How do Calvinists explain this contradiction to the perseverance of the saints?

In a June 14, 2009, blog entitled, "You Will Never Be Thirsty Again," John Piper discusses John 4:1-15. He says,

> Don't miss the five things he says about the water that he gives—and offers you today: 1)

It is the gift of God (v 10); 2) It's living water
(v 10); 3) If you drink it, you will never thirst
again—that is, it is always there to satisfy you
when your longing soul is thirsty (v 14); 4) This
water becomes a spring—a well of water (v 14).
That's why you will never be thirsty again—*not
because one drink is enough, but because one
drink produces a well for an eternity of drinks;*
5) This water gives eternal life (v 14) (emphasis
added).[27]

It is in his fourth point that Piper attempts to counter the idea that one drink forever quenches your thirst.
He specifically denies that one drink is enough. Instead,
he suggests that one drink causes you to keep on drinking forever.

Notice how Piper's fifth point contradicts the idea
that one must keep on drinking. Once one drinks this
water, he has eternal life: "This water gives eternal life."

While the woman was wrong to think that Jesus was
talking about physical water and physical life, she was
right that He was promising that one drink would forever quench her thirst. Notice that she said, "Sir, give me
this water, that I may not thirst, *nor come here to draw*"
(John 4:15). She would not need to bring her waterpot to
the well day after day to draw water.

In his *Systematic Theology*, Reymond comments
on the other verse in John's Gospel that picks up on
the theme of drinking living water, John 6:35. He says
"'Coming to him' and 'believing in him,' Jesus says,
relieves one's spiritual hunger and thirst (John 6:35).

---

[27] See http://www.desiringgod.org/messages/you-will-never-be-thirsty-again. Accessed July 21, 2017.

Accordingly, Jesus is not binding eternal life here to liturgical ordinance."[28] But if believing in Jesus means one has everlasting life now, then there can be no requirement of perseverance in faith or good works. Reymond's comments accurately reflect the text, but not Calvinism.

In a chapter entitled "Perseverance and Assurance" in his *Systematic Theology*, Frame cites John 6:35 to prove that "Clearly, God promises eternal life to all who receive Christ (John 1:12…6:35…)."[29] He goes on to say that while his name is not listed in the Bible explicitly, "my name is there *implicitly*."[30] He continues, "God promises salvation to *everybody* who believes. If you believe, then, that promise is yours. God promises to save *you*. And that promise is infallible, certain. You dare not doubt it."[31]

He adds an excellent warning about decisionism:

> This does not mean, of course, that anyone who raises his hand at an evangelistic meeting is saved. People sometimes do that hypocritically. Faith is an inward reality. But if it is there, you have a right to be assured. If you can honestly say, 'I am trusting Jesus for my salvation, not my own works, not my family, not my church, but Jesus,' then you can say without doubt that you are saved. And as we saw earlier in this chapter, you cannot lose that salvation.[32]

---

[28] Reymond, *A New Systematic Theology*, 964.

[29] Frame, *Systematic Theology*, 1004.

[30] Ibid., 1005, emphasis his.

[31] Ibid., emphasis his.

[32] Ibid.

While Frame does go on to say that there are other grounds of assurance (our growth in sanctification and the Spirit's inner testimony[33]) besides faith in the infallible and certain promise, the issue of assurance is already settled. Frame admits to certainty of his own eternal destiny since he believes the promise.

Frame's comments on assurance and on John 6:35 and other texts in John are insightful. However, they are not consistent with Calvinism.

John 4:13-15 is a showstopper for Calvinism.

The Basis of Condemnation Is Unbelief, Not Works (Revelation 20:15)

If the Calvinist doctrine of the perseverance of the saints were true, then we'd expect that at the Great White Throne Judgment we'd read, "Anyone who failed to endure in faith and good work was cast into the lake of fire." Yet we find that the issue is who is recorded in the Book of Life, not what is recorded in the books of deeds.

How Calvinists deal with Rev 20:15 shows the fragility of Calvinism.

John Piper published an article entitled, "What Will the Final Judgment Mean for You?" There he discusses Rev 20:11-15. He says,

> So how then does the record of our lives contained in 'the books' have a part in our judgment? The answer is that the books contain enough evidence of our belonging to Christ that they function as a public confirmation of our faith and our union with him... I do not

---

[33] Ibid., 1005-1006

mean that the record will contain more good
works than bad works. I mean that there will be
recorded there the kind of change that shows
the reality of faith—the reality of regeneration
and union with Christ. There will be enough
evidences…in the books to verify the born-
again reality of those written in the book of
life.[34]

The problem with this comment is that there is not
a hint of this in Rev 20:11-15. Indeed, what Piper says
essentially contradicts the clear statement of Rev 20:15,
"Anyone not found written in the Book of Life was cast
into the lake of fire." That verse shows that the sole basis
for condemnation or kingdom entrance is what's in the
Book of Life, not what's in the books of deeds.

In addition, what Piper says actually fails to teach the
Reformed doctrine of the perseverance of the saints. A
person might have "enough evidences in the books" from
works done prior to the time when the person fell away
from the faith. There was nothing in Piper's blog to assert
that one must persevere! Maybe that is because there is
nothing said about perseverance in Rev 20:11-15.

Revelation 20:11-15 contradicts Calvinism.

Assurance of Eternal Destiny Excludes
Required Perseverance (John 11:25-27)

Jesus told Martha about the resurrection of believers
and the eternal security of believers. But in His interaction with her, He indicated that anyone who believes in

---

[34] See http://www.desiringgod.org/articles/the-books-at-the-judgment.
Accessed July 17, 2017.

Jesus now will never die (John 11:26). But if Calvinism were true, shouldn't the Lord have said, "Anyone who lives and perseveres in faith and good works will never die"?

So how do Calvinists handle this passage?

In a sermon available at the Grace to You website, John MacArthur goes over these verses. He proclaims that Martha was a believer, and she knew it. Based on her testimony in John 11:27, MacArthur says, "She already believed."[35] He said, "She is an OT saint."[36] He indicates "everlasting life…is for anyone who believes."[37]

What is missing in his sermon is a statement that one must persevere in faith and good works in order to have everlasting life. But, of course, that would be to contradict the teaching of John 11:25-27. MacArthur says that Martha was eternally secure right then. Thus nothing could happen in the future to cause her to lose that life. She had everlasting life and she knew it. She knew her eternal destiny did not depend on her perseverance in faith or in good works.

John 11:25-27 is inconsistent with Calvinism.

---

[35] See https://www.gty.org/library/sermons-library/43-58/i-am-the-resurrection-and-the-life-part-1. Accessed August 21, 2017.
[36] Ibid.
[37] Ibid.

Election Concerns Service, Not Destiny

BECAUSE OF THE STRONG INFLUENCE OF CALVINISM in Evangelicalism today, the doctrine of election has been widely understood to concern one's eternal destiny. Those whom God elected will spend eternity with the Lord. Those whom God did not elect will spend eternity in the lake of fire.

There have always been people who questioned *on philosophical grounds* the Calvinist understanding of election. How could God be good if He created beings with no opportunity to escape an eternity of everlasting torment? Indeed, if we believe that only a small percentage of humanity will avoid eternal condemnation, as Calvinism teaches, then the goodness and fairness of God is even more in question. But this is a philosophical or theological approach, not a Biblical one.

In the Bible, election is not about eternal destiny but about service and eternal reward. God has chosen a nation, a city, a Person, and many individuals to serve and glorify Him both now and in the life to come.

Foreseen Faith Results in Election to Life

Jacobus Arminius didn't agree with the Calvinist view of election and predestination. He felt it was a fatalistic view that is "repugnant to the Nature of God" and "is at open hostility with the Nature of Eternal Life."[1]

A leading Arminian view is that God looked ahead to see which people He wanted to choose. He chose based on something in the people chosen, namely, their foreseen faith.[2]

In Arminianism, being regenerate does not necessarily mean that you are chosen. God only chooses those He foresees will *persevere* in faith (and good works) until death. Hence, it is possible for someone to believe in Jesus, to become regenerate, only to later stop believing and lose his salvation. That person would have been regenerate, but not chosen.

---

[1] Cited by Danilo Carvalho in "Jacobus Arminius' Contribution [to a] Christian Understanding of Salvation in Light of Christian Holiness" (http://dufreire.wordpress.com/2008/04/25/jacobus-arminius%E2%80%99-contribution-christian-understanding-of-salvation-in-light-of-christian-holiness/#_ftn17).

[2] See Kevin Jackson's article, "An Explanation of Simple Foreknowledge" at http://evangelicalarminians.org/?q=node/1285. Accessed July 10, 2017.

Corporate Election to Life

Some Arminians[3] and some who call themselves neither Calvinists nor Arminians hold to what is called *corporate election*. It is based in great part on Eph 1:4: "He chose us in Him before the foundation of the world."

Jesus is chosen. Therefore, whoever comes to faith in Jesus becomes chosen, too, because he is a part of the Body of Christ, the Church.

This view rejects the idea of individual election for eternal life. Instead, Jesus is chosen as the King and all who believe in Him become part of the body that will be in the kingdom of the King.

Election to Life Conditioned on Unknown Factors

According to modified Calvinism, God chose some and not others, but His choice was not arbitrary. Nor did He choose based on who would believe, since hypothetically everyone would believe if God kept turning up the heat.

Others posit a view of election that is somewhere between Calvinism and Arminianism. They suggest that God chose based on knowing the people in advance. His choice is based on many factors unknown to us. One of those factors may be the responsiveness of people to His drawing.[4]

---

[3] See http://evangelicalarminians.org/A-Concise-Summary-of-the-Corporate-View-of-Election-and-Predestination. Accessed July 10, 2017.
[4] See "Calvinism vs. Biblicism vs. Arminianism" at http://www.lostpinesbiblechurch.com/docs/Calvinism_Biblicism_Arminianism.pdf. Accessed July 21, 2017.

In this view God chose who would be born again, and the others were not chosen. But it does have some free will aspect to it since God takes us into account when choosing.

Election Is to Ministry

Over the past ten to fifteen years I've been studying the Biblical references to God's choosing and electing people. What I have found is far different from the Calvinist view of election I was taught at Dallas Theological Seminary.

When we study the Biblical words for election and choosing (*eklektos, eklegomai, eklogē, hairetizō, haireomai, suneklektos*), what we find is radically different from what is commonly taught about the Biblical doctrine of election. When the Bible teaches about God's choosing individuals, a nation, and even a city, it speaks of divine choice *for ministry*, not for eternal destiny. The Biblical doctrine of election is not about who will spend eternity with the Lord and who will not. It is about ministries that people are chosen to do for the Lord.

The Elect Are God's Chosen People, Israel (Matthew 24:22, 31)

We all know that Israel was God's chosen people. There is even a ministry to Jews today called *Chosen People Ministries*.

Yet we tend to think that Israel is only called *chosen* in the Old Testament (e.g., Deut 7:6; 14:2; 1 Kgs 3:8; Ps 33:12; 106:5; Isa 43:10; 45:4; 65:9, 22).

The New Testament refers to Israel as the elect in seven different passages. Two of those passages are found in the Olivet Discourse:

> [The Lord Jesus said] And unless those days were shortened, no flesh would be saved [i.e., would physically survive]; but *for the elect's sake* those days will be shortened" (Matt 24:22, emphasis added).

> And He will send His angels with a great sound of a trumpet, and *they will gather together His elect* from the four winds, from one end of heaven to the other (Matt 24:31, emphasis added).

The Jews were chosen to be the line through which Messiah came. Israel was chosen to serve God in its practices and in its worship. Indeed, God has not given up on Israel. By the end of the Tribulation Israel will cry out to the Lord Jesus and will be delivered. During the Millennium and then on the new earth, Israel will serve God forever in its practices and praise.

Due to the bias toward the Calvinist understanding of who *the elect* are, many of the references to Israel as *the elect* in the New Testament, including these two, are misunderstood. If the New Testament follows and is built upon the Old Testament, then it should not be surprising that both testaments refer to Israel as God's chosen, His elect.

Calvinists think that the Lord was talking about gathering all Church-Age believers together at the end of the age in Matt 24:31. But how can Matt 24:22 refer to Church-Age believers?

Why would it be vital for Church-Age believers to physically survive the seven-year Tribulation? Of course, we will be raptured before then (1 Thess 4:16-17). But even if we were to go through the Tribulation, why would it be necessary for our sake that some of us physically survive?

The point is that those days had to be kept to seven years and no more *for Israel's sake*. In order for God to fulfill promises made to Israel which have not yet been fulfilled, there must be Jewish people in natural bodies who go into the Millennium to raise up a glorious nation.

Obviously not all of the elect are born again, since most Jews today are unbelieving. Yet they are still the elect. That is, they are the people God chose to bear His name and His image and to live in His country and in His city.

The other five New Testament uses that refer to Israel as the elect are just as obvious if we simply study the contexts:

> "Unless the Lord had shortened those days, no flesh would be saved [i.e., would physically survive]; *but for the elect's sake, whom He chose,* He shortened the days" (Mark 13:20, emphasis added).

> Then the Lord said, "Hear what the unjust judge said. *And shall God not avenge His own elect who cry out day and night to Him,* though He bears long with them? I tell you that He will

avenge them speedily. Nevertheless, when the Son of Man comes, will He really find faith on the earth?" (Luke 18:6-8, emphasis added).

 And not only *this*, but when Rebecca also had conceived by one man, *even* by our father Isaac (for *the children* not yet being born, nor having done any good or evil, *that the purpose of God according to election might stand*, not of works but of Him who calls), it was said to her, "The older shall serve the younger." As it is written, "Jacob I have loved, but Esau I have hated" (Rom 9:10-13, emphasis added).

Concerning the gospel they [the Jews] are enemies for your sake, *but concerning the election they are beloved* for the sake of the fathers (Rom 11:28, emphasis added).

Remember that Jesus Christ, of the seed of David, was raised from the dead according to my gospel, for which I suffer trouble as an evildoer, even to the point of chains; but the word of God is not chained. Therefore I endure all things *for the sake of the elect*, that *they also* [Jews also] may obtain the salvation which is in Christ Jesus with eternal glory (2 Tim 2:8-10, emphasis added).

Jesus, God's Chosen Messiah and Savior

Jesus Himself is *the Chosen One, the Elect*. He was chosen by God the Father to be the chief cornerstone (1 Pet 2:4, 6), to be the Messiah (Isa 42:1-4; 49:7; Matt 12:18; Luke 9:35; 23:35; John 1:34), and to die on the cross for our sins (Matt 12:18; 1 Pet 2:4).

> Coming to Him as to a living stone, rejected indeed by men, but *chosen by God* (1 Pet 2:4, emphasis added).

> Behold, I lay in Zion *a chief cornerstone, elect*, precious, and he who believes *on Him* will by no means be put to shame (1 Pet 2:6, emphasis added).

Twelve Men Chosen as Christ's Apostles

Jesus chose twelve men to be His disciples and His apostles (Luke 6:13; John 6:70; 13:18; 15:16, 19; Acts 1:2). When one of those, Judas, betrayed Jesus, his place was taken by another man chosen by God, Matthias (Acts 1:24-26).

> And when it was day, He called His disciples to Himself; and from them *He chose twelve whom He also named apostles*…(Luke 6:13, emphasis added).

> [He had given commandments] *to the apostles whom He had chosen* (Acts 1:2, emphasis added).

> And they prayed and said, "You, O Lord, who
> know the hearts of all, *show which of these two*
> *You have chosen* to take part *in this ministry and*
> *apostleship* from which Judas by transgression
> fell, that he might go to his own place." And
> they cast their lots, and the lot fell on Matthias.
> And he was numbered with the eleven apostles
> (Acts 1:24-26, emphasis added).

Since Judas was one of the chosen disciples, yet was not born again, that shows that election is to service, not destiny. His place of service was taken by another.

Chosen Sojourners (1 Peter 1:2)

In his first epistle Peter wrote to Jewish believers scattered around the Roman Empire. He called them *elect* (or *chosen*) *sojourners*. Though many versions translate 1 Pet 1:2 as "*elect according to foreknowledge*," the word elect (*eklektos*) actually occurs in verse 1 immediately before *sojourners*:

> Peter, an apostle of Jesus Christ, *to the chosen*
> *pilgrims* of the Dispersion in Pontus, Galatia,
> Cappadocia, Asia, and Bithynia…(1 Pet 1:1, my
> own translation).

Many Other Types of Election As Well

Note the following types of election:
Saul was chosen to be the apostle to the Gentiles (Acts 9:15; 13:2; 22:14-15).

Peter was chosen to be the first to take the gospel to the Gentiles (Acts 15:7).

God chose Moses to be Israel's leader, and to deliver her out of Egypt (Num 16:5-6, 28-30).

God chose Levi to be the priestly line (Num 17:5; 1 Sam 2:28; 2 Chron 29:11).

Abraham (Neh 9:7), Isaac, Jacob (Ps 135:4; Isa 41:8; Ezek 20:5; Rom 9:10-13), and Judah (1 Chron 28:4; Ps 78:67) were all chosen to be ancestors of Messiah.

David was chosen to replace Saul as king (2 Sam 6:21; 1 Kgs 8:16; 1 Chron 28:4; 2 Chron 6:6; Ps 89:3).

Solomon was chosen to succeed David as king (1 Chron 29:1).

God chose Mary and Joseph to be Messiah's parents (Luke 1:30; Matt 1:20).

God chose Jerusalem to be Israel's capital and the New Jerusalem to be the world capital (e.g., Deut 15:20; 16:2, 15; 1 Kgs 8:44; 11:13; 14:21; 2 Kgs 21:7; 23:27; 2 Chron 6:6, 34; 12:13; 33:7; Neh 1:9; Ps 132:13; Zech 3:2; Rev 21:2, 24).

God chose all living Christians to be raptured before the Tribulation (1 Thess 5:8-10; 2 Thess 2:13).

God will choose Christians who persevere in faith and good works to rule with Christ (2 Pet 1:10-11).

Application

A wrong view of election eliminates assurance. If you think that God selects some to have everlasting life and that election is unknowable, as Calvinists teach, then you can't be sure of your eternal destiny until you die. That is a sad way to live.

Thus one application of the idea of election to service is that our assurance is based solely on the testimony of God concerning His Son (John 5:24; 1 John 5:9-13). Whoever believes in Jesus has everlasting life (John 3:16; 5:24; 6:35). It really is that simple. I'm assured because I believe the promise of life.

Knowing that God chooses us to serve Him should provide an additional motivation to get to work. He did not choose us to sit on the sidelines and watch the angels serve Him forever. God chose us to serve Him now and forever.

In addition, we can and should rejoice because we know the Chosen One. The Lord Jesus is the One God chose. And the Lord Jesus fulfilled His ministry. He lived a sinless life and He died on the cross, taking away the sin of the world (John 1:29; 1 John 2:2). His triumphant cry, "It is finished!" (John 19:30), is directly related to the Biblical doctrine of election. He was chosen to go to the cross for us and He did. The finished work of Christ is the finished work of the Chosen One.

Conclusion

God elects people and places for service. He does not elect, as far as I can tell, anyone to everlasting life.

Of course, God has decided that all who believe in Jesus for everlasting life will be in His glorious kingdom forever. And He has determined that all who fail to believe in His Son will be eternally condemned. But God didn't choose who would believe and who would not.

Eternal destiny is simply a matter of who ends up in the Book of Life (Rev 20:15). All who believe in Jesus for His promise of life are in the Book and have everlasting life. All who die never having believed in Jesus are not in the Book and will not ever be in the Book (assuming they lived beyond the age of accountability and with full mental faculties).

The Biblical teaching on election does not support Calvinism's teaching on election. In the Bible, election is to service, not to eternal destiny.[5]

---

[5] For a defense of the vocational view of election see Shawn Lazar, *Chosen to Serve: Why Election Is to Service, Not to Eternal Life* (Denton, TX: Grace Evangelical Society, 2017).

Scripture Index

Subject Index

Bob Wilkin has a B.S. in Biology from U.C. Irvine. He also has a Ph.D. in New Testament from Dallas Theological Seminary. He has served as an evangelist, hospital chaplain, Bible college professor, pastor, and, since 1987, the founder and director of Grace Evangelical Society (GES). He has written several books, including *Confident in Christ*, *The Ten Most Misunderstood Words in the Bible*, *Inerrancy for Dummies*, and *A Gospel of Doubt*.

Bob regularly speaks across the country and internationally.

His hobbies include competitive racewalking, duplicate bridge (Silver Life Master), reading, and science fiction.

He and his wife Sharon live in Highland Village, Texas, a suburb of Dallas.

GRACE IN FOCUS is a free, bimonthly magazine about the gospel, assurance, and related issues.

You will read powerful testimonies, insightful Biblical studies, and encouraging practical lessons on living for Christ.

You will especially be presented with a clear saving message of faith alone, in Christ alone, for everlasting life that cannot be lost.

For your free U.S. subscription sign up at www.faithalone.org or send your name and address to P.O. Box 1308, Denton, TX 76202.

www.faithalone.org

Made in the USA
Monee, IL
27 October 2022